Running Press Kids
Hachette Book Group
1290 Avenue of the Americas, New York, NY 10104
www.runningpress.com/rpkids
@RP_Kids

Printed in Singapore

Originally published in 2022
by Quercus Editions Ltd,
a Hachette UK company, in Great Britain

First U.S. Edition: March 2022

Published by Running Press Kids, an imprint of
Perseus Books, LLC, a subsidiary of Hachette Book
Group, Inc. The Running Press Kids name and logo
is a trademark of the Hachette Book Group.

The Hachette Speakers Bureau provides a wide range
of authors for speaking events. To find out more, go to
www.hachettespeakersbureau.com or call (866) 376-6591.

The publisher is not responsible for websites
(or their content) that are not owned by the publisher.

Illustrations by Quinton Winter.
Cover design by TK.
Interior design by Sarah Green.

Library of Congress Control Number: 2021943445

ISBNs: 978-0-7624-7914-6 (hardcover),
978-0-7624-7915-3 (ebook)

1010

10 9 8 7 6 5 4 3 2 1

DARE ~to be~ DIFFERENT

INSPIRATIONAL WORDS FROM PEOPLE WHO CHANGED THE WORLD

Ben Brooks

THE GLOBAL BESTSELLING AUTHOR OF
STORIES FOR BOYS WHO DARE TO BE DIFFERENT

ILLUSTRATED BY QUINTON WINTER

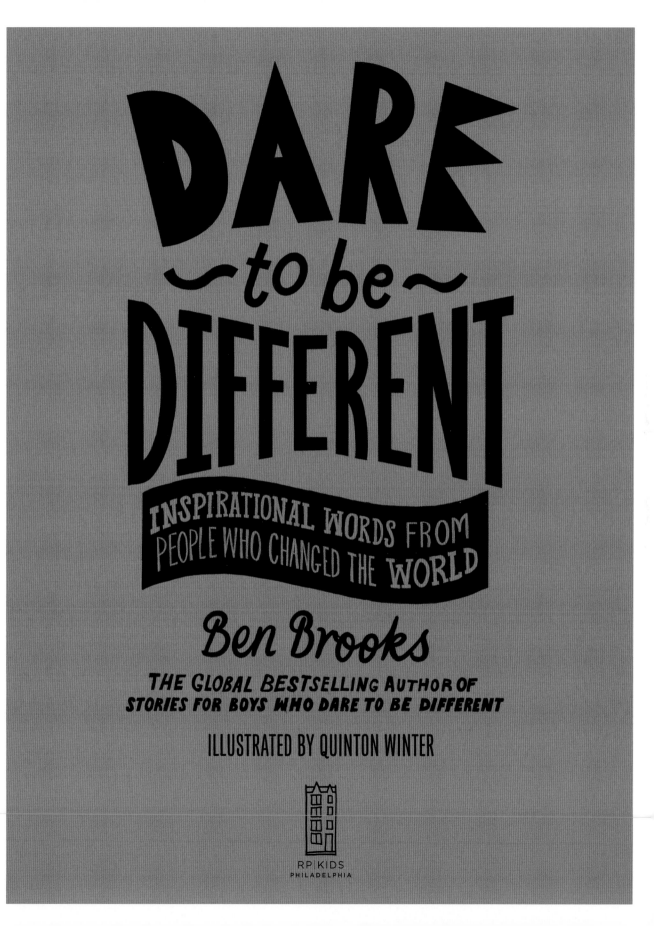

RP|KIDS
PHILADELPHIA

CONTENTS

JAY ABDO

(BORN 1962)

Jay was one of the biggest actors in the Middle East. Millions of people in the Arabic-speaking world knew him from his films. But life wasn't easy. In Syria, where Jay is from, it was growing increasingly difficult to criticize the people in charge. Jay was asked to speak out in support of the government on TV. When he refused, they started to harass and threaten him.

Jay secretly met up with a journalist from America and explained to her what was going on in Syria. The publication of the article put Jay's life in danger. He fled to America, where his wife and children were already living.

In America, nobody knew who he was. He hadn't been able to bring any of his money with him when he moved, so he took a job delivering pizza just to make enough to cover the bills.

Jay didn't give up on acting. He went to every audition he could, determined to find even the smallest part. Eventually, his hard work paid off, and he was given a big role in a film called *Queen of the Desert*. How did he do it?

"PATIENCE, PATIENCE, PATIENCE. AND FOCUS. I CAME FROM BEING IN THE TOP OF MY LEAGUE AS AN ACTOR IN MY COUNTRY, TO A PLACE WHERE NOBODY KNEW ME. I STARTED WITH ANY PARTS I COULD GET BY AUDITIONING, EVEN FOR A TWO-LINE PART. YOU HAVE TO HAVE A 'DO WHATEVER IT TAKES' ATTITUDE."

Jay starred in the film with one of the most famous Hollywood stars in existence, Nicole Kidman. When Jay and Nicole went to film at a market in Morocco, she was amazed to see that more of the people swarming around them recognized Jay than her. "Are these fans of yours?" she asked Jay. He told her they were, that to Arabic-speakers, he was very famous.

Jay proved that even when it might feel as though you've lost everything, it is always possible to come back. Nothing is permanent. We all go through ups and downs; it's just a matter of refusing to believe that the downs will last forever.

LOUISA MAY ALCOTT

(1832–1888)

In 1868, Louisa's novel, *Little Women*, was published in America. The first edition of 2,000 copies sold out so quickly that the publisher rushed to print more. Thousands and thousands of people fell in love with the four March sisters in the story: Jo, Meg, Beth, and Amy. Readers felt almost as though the girls were their own friends and sisters.

Louisa herself had grown up as one of four sisters. Their father, Amos, would drag them around the country as he carried out plans he hoped would change their lives. He tried opening schools that focused on what the students wanted to learn. That failed. He tried starting a community that lived off the land and refused to buy anything made by enslaved people. That failed too.

When Louisa started writing, she wrote all kinds of books, including fairy tales, horror stories, comedies, and romances. She wrote under many different names and found some success, though it was nothing compared to what was to come.

One year, Louisa's father asked a big publishing house if they would put out his philosophy book. The editor, Thomas Niles, said that he would publish the book only if Amos could convince Louisa to write a story for girls. Louisa wasn't sure at first. She said she didn't really know anything about girls or what they wanted.

In the end, she started turning the story of her own life with her sisters into a book. That book became *Little Women*, which has since sold millions of copies and been turned into countless plays, films, and TV shows. In chapter four of the book, the youngest sister, Amy, tells her husband:

"I AM NOT AFRAID OF STORMS, FOR I AM LEARNING HOW TO SAIL MY SHIP."

Amy knew that it's impossible to learn how to really sail on smooth, still waters. It's in storms that we learn the most important lessons of all; it's the difficult times that truly teach us how to sail our ships. It turned out that all of the hard things her family had been through were what enabled Louisa to write a story that has gone on to mean so much to so many.

JULIE ANDREWS

(BORN 1935)

Julie's parents split up when she was very young. At first, Julie lived with her father, but she later moved in with her mother and stepfather. The family were poor. Rats lived in the pipes of their house.

Both of her parents worked as performers and it became clear that Julie would follow in their footsteps. She had a beautiful voice and audiences went wild when they heard her sing.

In fact, her performances were so successful that it wasn't long before Julie was the one earning the money for her family. She was cast in a West End show, where someone who worked for Disney spotted her. They were working on a film and thought that Julie would be perfect for the main part.

That role was Mary Poppins. It would turn Julie into an actress who was known and loved around the world.

Then, in 1965, Julie played the lead part in a film based on a musical by Richard Rodgers and Oscar Hammerstein. The film was called *The Sound of Music* and it told the true story of the von Trapps, a family of singers living in Austria just as the world was on the verge of descending into war. The film was so successful, it broke records in twenty-nine countries.

One song in particular proved very popular. In it, Julie sang:

"WHEN THE DOG BITES, WHEN THE BEE STINGS, WHEN I'M FEELING SAD— I SIMPLY REMEMBER MY FAVORITE THINGS AND THEN I DON'T FEEL SO BAD."

Some years later, after surgery on her throat, Julie found that she'd lost her singing voice. She didn't let that slow her down. She wrote children's books, acted in films, and even gave her voice to the queen in *Shrek*. As Julie sung in *The Sound of Music*, when life gets difficult, it's important to remember the things that mean the most to us. Whether it's friends, family, ice cream, or football, there's always something that can be a light in times of darkness.

JANE AUSTEN

(1775–1817)

Jane's family loved reading aloud to each other. She first started writing just to make her siblings and parents laugh. The Austens were a big family. Jane had six brothers and one sister and they lived together in a sleepy English village called Steventon.

When she was a teenager, Jane would fill notebooks with her stories. One of these notebooks contained a tale called "Love and Friendship," in which Jane made fun of the typical romance novels of the time by exaggerating the way the women talked and acted. In the book, the character Sophie is dying of consumption, and as she is on her deathbed, she gives this advice to her friend Laura:

"RUN MAD AS OFTEN AS YOU CHOOSE, BUT DO NOT FAINT!"

It would be many years before anyone outside of Jane's family would read those words. Her first published novel was written later, when Jane was in her twenties. She paid with her own money to have it printed. The first 750 copies of *Sense and Sensibility* were put together and they very quickly sold out.

The books didn't even have Jane's name on the cover. Instead, they simply said "by a lady." We don't know exactly why

Jane chose to publish her books anonymously, but many people believe it was because at the time, it might have been considered wrong for a woman to make money through her own writing.

It was only after she'd died that Jane's work became truly popular. Her novels have now sold millions of copies and been turned into countless films and TV shows (including a zombie version of her most famous work, titled *Pride and Prejudice and Zombies*). Though her books are set in what feels like the distant past, the emotions of love and heartbreak, jealousy and anger, hope and disappointment are all too familiar, no matter which century you're living in.

Despite not achieving much success in her lifetime, Jane lived how Sophie encouraged Laura to live: she let her ideas and her passions run wild and she refused to ever give up.

The notebooks Jane wrote in as a teenager now have pride of place in Oxford's Bodleian Library and the British Museum. Hundreds of thousands of fans flock to see them every year.

LAYNE BEACHLEY

(BORN 1972)

As a baby, Layne was adopted by a family called the Beachleys. She was eight years old when she found out that they weren't her biological parents. Though the Beachleys loved Layne very much, she couldn't help feeling like someone hadn't wanted her. She dreamed of becoming a world champion. That way, she thought, everyone would love her.

It turned out Layne had both a talent and a passion for surfing. She dedicated hours to riding waves on the beach of her home in Manly, Australia. Though most surfers were men, Layne competed fearlessly against them, refusing to let anyone's expectations hold her down.

At sixteen, Layne took part in her first professional competition. She then spent over twenty years traveling the planet, riding huge waves on beautiful beaches. She's surfed waves twice the size of houses, and often found herself with broken bones and stitches as a result. But her injuries couldn't hold her back, and neither could the fact that some men thought surfing wasn't a sport that was meant for women.

How did she do it? Layne says:

〰〰〰〰〰〰〰〰〰〰

"DON'T FEEL LIKE YOU HAVE TO FIT IN: BECAUSE ONCE YOU TRY AND FIT INTO SOMETHING—ESPECIALLY IF IT'S

AN ENVIRONMENT WHERE YOU DON'T FEEL LIKE YOU TRULY BELONG—THEN YOU'RE COMPROMISING ON YOUR OWN VALUES AND YOUR OWN BELIEFS."

〰〰〰〰〰〰〰〰〰〰

Layne refused to do what others expected of her. She proudly stood up and stood out, becoming one of the greatest surfers in the world. In fact, she's the only surfer in history to have won six world titles in a row.

In 2008, Layne retired from professional surfing. But that didn't mean her work was done. Through her charity, Aim for the Stars, Layne now encourages and supports young girls to fight for their dreams. As she said, Layne doesn't want anyone to have to compromise on their values or beliefs, because when that happens, we lose who we really are. Layne wants all the kids who admire her to know that they don't have to worry about how they look to others; they just have to be themselves.

TATIANA BILBAO

(BORN 1972)

One of Tatiana's buildings is an aquarium on the coast of Mexico, designed to look like an ancient shipwreck. Another is a spaceship-like exhibition pavilion in Jinhuan Park, China. And one is a house that only costs $8,000 to construct, meaning it can be used to provide a safe, comfortable, dignified home for families who may not otherwise have anywhere to live.

Tatiana had been drawn to designing buildings from an early age. She came from a family of architects. When she received a Barbie as a present, Tatiana set about building a city for it to live in. She studied architecture at university and then went on to start designing real cities, while working for the urban housing department of Mexico City. During her time working for the government, Tatiana came to understand that Mexico didn't have enough houses, especially for poorer families. Most low-cost housing that existed also tended to be crowded, drab, and unpleasant to live in. Tatiana was determined to do something about it. She was convinced that:

> ### "YOU DON'T ONLY NEED TO BE AGAINST THINGS, YOU NEED TO PROPOSE A SOLUTION."

So when Tatiana left the government, she started her own architecture firm: Tatiana Bilbao Estudio. The studio took on a number of expensive, luxury commissions, and used the funds to work on projects that could help poorer people. The $8,000 house was Tatiana's proposed solution to the housing shortage. It is a flexible type of house, which can be easily changed to suit the number of people living in it, or even to adapt to the climate. The houses and their materials are handmade, rather than being created by machines, which helps to provide jobs in Mexico, where they're very much needed.

As Tatiana saw, it is easy to criticize or point out the things that aren't working. It is much harder, and much more useful, to find ways of changing them for the better.

ELIF BILGIN

(BORN 1997)

As a child growing up in Istanbul, Elif loved coming up
with inventions. She created windshield wipers for
her glasses, a tiny car that was powered by wind, and a
method for growing plants without soil. She knew
that the best inventions were ones that solved problems.

And Elif had stumbled on a big problem.

Petroleum-based plastic is a kind of
plastic that is often used for making
anything from drinking bottles to
sunglasses. The problem with it is
that the plastic doesn't break down,
so it ends up polluting the environment
and adding poisonous chemicals to
our water and food. When Elif realized
that thousands of tons of banana peels
were being thrown away every year,
she had an idea. What if she could find
a way of turning those banana peels
into plastic?

Elif spent two years conducting experiments to try and devise a way of turning
the fruit skins into something useful.
Most of them failed, but eventually
she discovered a way of producing a
kind of plastic that could be used to
cover electrical cables. Despite only
being sixteen, Elif had found a way of
turning trash into something truly
useful. She thinks other kids are capable
of such remarkable discoveries too,
and says that:

> "I DON'T THINK THAT IT IS YOUR AGE THAT
> DETERMINES THE POTENTIAL YOU HAVE, IT IS THE
> UNLIMITED IMAGINATION YOU HAVE THAT GIVES
> YOU THE UNLIMITED POTENTIAL TO CREATE."

Her discovery earned Elif a "Science
in Action" prize, as well as making her
a finalist at the Google Science Fair.
The prize money will help Elif with
accomplishing her dream of becoming
a doctor, though that doesn't mean she's
going to give up inventing.

While studying in college, Elif had the
chance to intern at Virgin Galactic, a
company that is trying to create the first
fleet of craft that will take tourists into
space. She helped design the passenger
seats for VSS *Unity*, an eight-seater
spaceship that has already completed
test flights to the edge of outer space.

Elif has proven that it's not how old
we are that counts; it's how big we're
willing to dream.

BJØRNSTJERNE BJØRNSON

(1832–1910)

Whenever a Norwegian athlete wins a competition, they sing a song called "Yes, We Love This Country" written by Bjørnstjerne Bjørnson back in the 1860s. Although Norway didn't actually have an official national anthem until 2019, when it came time to choose one, it was Bjørnstjerne's piece that was picked.

Bjørnstjerne had been writing poems since he was eleven. He lived with his parents and five siblings in a remote village called Kvikne, which was spread out between the river Orkla and steep mountains covered in lush green trees. He was sent away to a school in a larger town when he turned seventeen. There, he met other writers, like Henrik Ibsen, who would all go on to shape the future of the country with their words.

Norway had become independent from the neighboring country of Denmark in 1814, although it remained united with its other neighbor, Sweden. Bjørnstjerne wrote plays, poems, and stories that celebrated his country's own history and people, rather than the culture of its neighbors.

That didn't necessarily mean he wanted his country to stand alone. When the time came to decide whether they would remain united with Sweden, a rumor spread that Bjørnstjerne had sent the prime minister a telegram that read "Now is the time to unite." According to the rumor, the prime minister sent a reply that said "Now is the time to shut up."

Bjørnstjerne tried to see the good in the world. He once wrote:

"DO NOT COMPLAIN BENEATH THE STARS ABOUT THE LACK OF BRIGHT SPOTS IN YOUR LIFE."

As Bjørnstjerne had learned, there are always things of beauty and goodness in the world, but if we spend our time complaining, we won't see them. It's up to us to tilt our heads back and open our eyes. It's up to us to notice the bright spots in our lives.

JULIA BLUHM

(BORN 1998)

Every day, thousands of photographs of people are published online, on TV, and in magazines. Many of these photos are not telling the truth. After being taken, they're edited on computers, to get rid of fat or wrinkles, or just change the shape of someone's body. The results often look more like dolls than human beings.

When Julia realized this, she was horrified. She was a fifteen-year-old ballet dancer and understood how damaging this kind of editing could be to girls like her. If the photos in the magazines she read weren't real, then of course she was never going to feel comfortable in her own skin, because she would never be able to look like the models she was seeing.

Julia started a campaign to raise awareness among young women that the photographs they see are often not honest. She also started a petition to try and convince one of her favorite magazines, *Seventeen,* to start featuring pictures of real women that hadn't been altered by computers.

The petition received over 80,000 signatures. Julia presented the results in the form of a protest outside the magazine's headquarters. She and the other protestors demanded that if a magazine was supposed to be for girls like them, then

it should contain pictures of girls who actually looked like them. Eventually the editor of the magazine published an issue in which she promised that the magazine would stop changing the shapes of girls' faces and bodies. Julia had won her fight.

Her advice for other young people is:

"QUESTION THE MEDIA . . . SAY, THAT'S NOT REALISTIC, THE GIRLS IN MY SCHOOL OR TOWN DON'T LOOK LIKE THAT."

By questioning the pictures that were put in front of her, Julia came to realize that it wasn't her who was wrong, it was the media. By standing up against what was going on, she has helped numerous young girls to understand that they're beautiful as they are.

BERTA CÁCERES

(1971–2016)

The Lenca are a group of people who come from parts of Middle America now known as Honduras and El Salvador. They have lived on the land for thousands of years, though their numbers started to fall when the Spanish arrived in 1519, bringing violence and disease with them. Life for the Lenca has been difficult ever since.

Berta's mother was a governor, a mayor, and a midwife who cared for thousands of poor Lenca people. Berta saw from a young age how badly her fellow tribe members were treated by the governments who were supposed to look out for them.

When Berta turned twenty-two, she founded a group who aimed to stand up against all the politicians and companies who put money before the rights of the Lenca people. They fought illegal logging, pollution, mining, destructive construction projects, and military bases put on Lenca land.

In 2009, construction started in Honduras on a huge hydroelectric dam. The project would make it difficult for many Lenca to access food and water, as well as putting their traditional ways of life at risk. Despite this, they weren't even asked before building started. Berta led protests against the dam, including organizing groups of people to occupy land and prevent work from continuing. The police threatened, harassed, and even shot at them. But they refused to surrender. Eventually construction moved somewhere else. Berta told people:

"LET US COME TOGETHER AND MOVE FORWARD WITH HOPE AS WE DEFEND AND CARE FOR THE EARTH AND ITS SPIRITS."

Berta saw that the problems we are faced with today will only be solved if we can find a way of uniting as one people. If we continue to fight among ourselves, we will only end up destroying the earth as well as each other. If, however, we can come together, we will be able to look after the planet we call home and exist peacefully, side by side.

Tragically, Berta was shot and killed for getting in the way of so many powerful people. Her daughter, Bertha Zúñiga, continues to fight for the rights of the Lenca today.

JOSÉ RAÚL CAPABLANCA

(1888–1942)

One afternoon, in Havana, Cuba, José sat watching his father play chess with a neighbor. He pointed out that his father had made a wrong move.

"If you're so good," his father grumbled, "then why don't we play a game?"

So they played. And José won.

It soon became clear that José had a natural talent for the game. By the age of eight, he was winning most of his games at the Havana chess club. At twelve, he won the Cuban national championship.

In 1914, when José was twenty-six, the best chess players in the world were invited to a tournament in St. Petersburg, Russia. Over a month in spring, José played against ten of the greatest players ever to have lived, and it seemed as though he was winning. Then José came up against Dr. Emanuel Lasker, the world champion at the time. Emanuel was a mathematician and a philosopher from Germany who sometimes made bad moves to confuse his opponents. That day, he played such a complex and surprising game that José lost. The boy from Havana came second in the tournament.

It was a painful defeat but José knew that didn't mean he had failed. He once said:

ᐯᐯᐯᐯᐯᐯᐯᐯᐯᐯᐯᐯᐯᐯᐯ

"YOU MAY LEARN MUCH MORE FROM A GAME YOU LOSE THAN FROM A GAME YOU WIN. YOU WILL HAVE TO LOSE HUNDREDS OF GAMES BEFORE BECOMING A GOOD PLAYER."

ᐯᐯᐯᐯᐯᐯᐯᐯᐯᐯᐯᐯᐯᐯᐯ

After that tournament, José would go on to win most of the games he played. He would eventually play Dr. Lasker again and beat him, quite easily, becoming the world champion.

José is still remembered as one of the greatest chess players of all time. He knew that often we learn much more from things going wrong than we do from things going right. And if we learn from failure, then we haven't failed at all, because we've grown as a person, becoming even stronger in the process.

LYDIA MARIA CHILD

(1802–1880)

As a child, Lydia was greatly inspired by her parents, who showed great kindness to their poorer neighbors in the town of Medford, Massachusetts.

When Lydia's older brother suggested that she try to write a book, she wrote *Hobomok*, the story of a Native American hero who falls in love with a white woman. She would spend the rest of her life using her words to make a difference.

In 1826, Lydia published what many people consider to be the first magazine just for kids. *Juvenile Miscellany* included stories, puzzles, articles, and jokes, as well as pieces about the ways in which the native people of North and South America had been treated so brutally by the invaders who had come from across the ocean.

It was very popular. Children would sit out on their doorsteps, waiting for the newest issue of the magazine to arrive. Kids loved the stories and Lydia came to love her readers too.

But the magazine was only part of Lydia's work. She also fought for the freedom of enslaved black people. By 1830, there were over two million black enslaved people in America, a number that would keep increasing until the end of the Civil War in 1865.

By 1834, Lydia's work fighting against slavery meant that people called her a troublemaker and stopped buying her books. Angry parents also canceled their children's subscriptions to *Juvenile Miscellany*. Lydia sent out her last issue of the magazine, featuring a letter in which she said goodbye to her readers. She wrote:

"MAY GOD BLESS YOU, MY YOUNG FRIENDS, AND IMPRESS DEEPLY UPON YOUR HEARTS THE CONVICTION THAT ALL TRUE EXCELLENCE AND HAPPINESS CONSISTS IN LIVING FOR OTHERS, NOT FOR YOURSELVES."

Lydia lost her career because she refused to back down from what she knew was right. She believed that her life would be better spent helping others than helping herself, and that is why many still remember her as a hero today.

CROWFOOT

(1830–1890)

As a boy, Crowfoot was given the name Astohkomi, or Shot Close, by the other members of his Native American tribe. When his father was killed and his mother got married again, he was given another name: Kyi-i-staah, or Bear Ghost. He eventually became known as Crowfoot after displaying great bravery in battle.

Like many Native American teenagers, Crowfoot would often go with older members of his group to raid and fight with neighboring tribes. He soon came to see how violent such excursions were. By the age of twenty, Crowfoot had fought in nineteen battles and been wounded many times. There was a lead ball still lodged in the back of his head from where he'd been shot.

Wars were raging between Native Americans and the white settlers who had come from over the ocean. Vicious, bloody battles took place, in which many people died. By the year 1900, over 90 percent of the Native Americans who had been living in the US when the settlers arrived would be dead. The few who were left were mainly herded into reservations like cattle.

Despite the violence and deceit shown by many of the settlers to Native Americans, Crowfoot tried to maintain peaceful relationships with them. He had already seen enough slaughter and wanted to do everything in his power to keep his tribe

safe. He signed a treaty that kept his people's right to hunt on their land, while ensuring that the British would pay them and provide them with certain foods, like flour and beef, in return for being able to use the area.

Before he passed away, Crowfoot shared one last piece of wisdom:

"WHAT IS LIFE? IT IS THE FLASH OF A FIREFLY IN THE NIGHT. IT IS THE BREATH OF A BUFFALO IN THE WINTERTIME. IT IS THE LITTLE SHADOW WHICH RUNS ACROSS THE GRASS AND LOSES ITSELF IN THE SUNSET."

Crowfoot had come to see that the most important, special moments of life were not the big victories or the grand events—they were the small moments of beauty that often go unnoticed as we hurry through our busy days.

MARIE CURIE

(1867–1934)

When Marie was a teenager in Warsaw, Poland, she attended a secret school, known as the Flying University. As the Russians who had occupied Poland didn't allow certain subjects to be taught, people learned in secret, with teachers holding lessons in private houses that were always changing location so that they could never be found.

The occupation wasn't the first hardship Marie had faced. She was just ten when her mother died. Three years after that, her older sister passed away too. But no matter what happened, Marie was determined not to let it get in the way of achieving her goals. She once said that:

> "LIFE IS NOT EASY FOR ANY OF US. BUT WHAT OF THAT? WE MUST HAVE PERSEVERANCE AND, ABOVE ALL, CONFIDENCE IN OURSELVES. WE MUST BELIEVE THAT WE ARE GIFTED FOR SOMETHING, AND THAT THIS THING, AT WHATEVER COST, MUST BE ATTAINED."

And Marie did. She eventually left Poland for Paris, where she studied math and physics at the famous Sorbonne University. That was where she met Pierre Curie and fell in love. Working together, Marie and Pierre discovered two entirely new chemical elements: polonium and radium. These would prove vital in the creation of X-rays.

By finding a way for doctors to see into the bodies of their patients, treating them became a much easier task. The work of Marie and her husband saved many lives.

Marie also volunteered during the First World War and drove ambulances to the front lines to rescue wounded soldiers. There, she trained many doctors and nurses in how best to make use of X-rays.

Throughout her career, Marie faced a lot of pain and hardship simply for being a woman in science at a time when most scientists were men. Despite her achievements, for example, Marie was never elected to the French Academy of Sciences.

But, as Marie said, we must push forward and we must have confidence in ourselves, regardless of how hard life gets. That is how we achieve the things we are destined to do.

DAVID DEUTSCH

(BORN 1953)

Quantum computers make use of some of the most mysterious forces in physics. They harness particles even smaller than atoms in order to solve complex problems. These computers might, at some point, even be able to solve certain problems that normal computers would never be capable of.

David moved from Israel to the UK as a young child and went on to become one of the key figures in quantum computing. He now lives on the outskirts of Oxford, in a house that is known for being wildly messy, filled with open books and scraps of paper covered in scribbled-down thoughts. David has a lot of ideas that other people find difficult to comprehend. He believes, for example, that there is an endless number of different universes alongside our own— some similar, and some much less so.

It's the kind of idea that can give you a headache. David realizes that thinking too hard for too long about how big the universe is can be scary, but he doesn't think we should feel small and irrelevant:

"FEELING INSIGNIFICANT BECAUSE THE UNIVERSE IS LARGE HAS EXACTLY THE SAME LOGIC AS FEELING INADEQUATE FOR NOT BEING A COW. OR A HERD OF COWS. THE UNIVERSE IS NOT THERE TO OVERWHELM US;

IT IS OUR HOME, AND OUR RESOURCE. THE BIGGER THE BETTER."

As a scientist, David expands his knowledge of the world by observing what's going on around him and trying to come up with explanations. He also believes that this is the best way to educate children. To support this idea, he founded a method of raising kids known as Taking Children Seriously. In his opinion, children shouldn't be forced to do things that they don't want to do. They should be free to follow their own curiosities and interests, wherever they may lead. In David's opinion, making us all sit through the same lessons at the same time is never going to be helpful, because we're all so different. We all have different strengths, passions, talents, and things to offer the world.

Like David said, you are not a cow, or a herd of cows. You are a person in a vast, mysterious universe, and it is entirely up to you how you want to find your way through it.

EDSGER W. DIJKSTRA

(1930–2002)

In 1957, when Edsger was getting married, he was asked to write his job on the documents. He wrote "computer programmer." The Dutch authorities told him he had to change it because no such job existed. He wrote "physicist" instead.

It had almost been true. When Edsger was younger, he went to university in the Netherlands to study physics. One year, however, he traveled to England for a summer school in computer programming at Cambridge, and realized he'd discovered the thing he wanted to dedicate his life to.

Edsger would spend the rest of his life bringing computers and programming out of laboratories and universities and into the homes of people around the world.

At the time, there were many problems that lay at the heart of computer engineering. One was known as the dining philosophers' problem, illustrated by the idea of five philosophers sitting around a table, each with a bowl of rice in front of them, and a chopstick on either side. The question was how they could all eat without anyone going hungry. Edsger proposed that the philosophers take it in turns using two chopsticks. It may not sound like much, but this solution changed the way that people approached computing. Edsger once explained that:

"TESTING SHOWS THE PRESENCE, NOT THE ABSENCE, OF BUGS."

What Edsger had discovered was true not just of computers, but of people too. Bugs, or weaknesses in a system, are only shown during difficult tests. And the tests aren't run to show that you have created something perfect, but to find ways you can improve what you do have. In the same way, when we go through difficult times, we can learn to spot our own weaknesses and pinpoint the things we could focus our energies on getting better at. We should never feel as though we've somehow failed because we have a few bugs. Every person, like every computer program, will have their own strengths and their own weaknesses. It's up to you what you do with them.

MAX EHRMANN

(1872–1945)

Max's parents were from Germany, but he was born in the small American town of Terra Haute, Indiana. There, Max lived a quiet life. He worked in law for a while, then joined his family's meatpacking business, and even started a company that made overalls.

When he got a little older, Max retired from work to focus on what he most loved to do: writing. One year, Max wrote a poem called "Desiderata," which he copied on to Christmas cards and sent out to his friends. It was a hopeful poem, packed with advice for how to live happily. One of these friends showed it to the doctor who was helping her deal with her sadness. The doctor printed 1,000 copies and sent them to soldiers who were fighting in the Second World War.

After that, the poem lay forgotten.

Max died in 1945 and was buried in the Terra Haute cemetery. Over twenty years later, a famous politician passed away and a copy of "Desiderata" was found in his house. This made the poem famous. Soon, Max's words were everywhere, from poetry collections to posters, from songs to films. Part of the poem reads:

"BE GENTLE WITH YOURSELF. YOU ARE A CHILD OF THE UNIVERSE NO LESS THAN THE TREES AND THE STARS; YOU HAVE A RIGHT TO BE HERE. AND WHETHER OR NOT IT IS CLEAR TO YOU, NO DOUBT THE UNIVERSE IS UNFOLDING AS IT SHOULD."

Sixty-five years after he'd died, the citizens of Max's town put up a statue and a bench in his honor, where people could go to think on the meaning behind "Desiderata": that no matter how rich, powerful, or famous some people might be, we are all just as meaningful as each other. We should remember to be kind to one another but, just as importantly, we should remember to be kind to ourselves.

RALPH WALDO EMERSON

(1803–1882)

When Ralph's wife, Ellen, died of consumption at the age of just twenty, his life was turned upside down. He quit his job as a priest and went in search of meaning.

He traveled around Europe, meeting some of the most famous poets of the age, like William Wordsworth and Samuel Taylor Coleridge. He forged connections with wild creatures and natural landscapes. He came up with some ideas of his own about what it truly means to be alive.

Ralph believed that humans and nature are the same, that nature isn't something that is separate from us, but something we are a part of. He also believed that even though we're all connected, we're all unique too.

They were ideas Ralph would carry with him for the rest of his life. He spread them across the world as he became more and more well known as a wise man, a kind man, and a great writer.

When Ralph had a daughter with his second wife, Lidian, they decided to name her after his first love: Ellen. As a young woman, Ellen was sent away to boarding school, but Ralph kept in touch with her by letters. In one, he wrote:

- - - - - - - - - - - - - - - - - - - -

"FINISH EVERY DAY, AND BE DONE WITH IT . . .
SOME BLUNDERS AND ABSURDITIES
NO DOUBT CREPT IN, FORGET THEM AS FAST
AS YOU CAN, TOMORROW IS A NEW DAY.
YOU SHALL BEGIN IT WELL AND SERENELY."

- - - - - - - - - - - - - - - - - - - -

Hopefully, Ellen managed to take her father's advice and find a way of leaving her mistakes behind so that she could move forward. There's no one in the world who doesn't do or say the wrong thing sometimes—what matters is that we manage to learn from our blunders and let them go.

Ralph knew, from losing his first wife at such a young age, that none of us ever know what the future holds. That's why it's so important to treasure what we have and to start each day with hope and joy.

VIGDÍS FINNBOGADÓTTIR

(BORN 1930)

In the year 1980, the whole of Iceland looked on nervously as its election votes were counted. It was an incredibly close race. Finally, the counting was over and the results came in: Vigdís had won. She was to become the president of Iceland and the first elected female head of state in history.

Vigdís hadn't always wanted to be a politician. Before running for election, she had taught French on Icelandic television, been a director in the theater, and worked as a tour guide, taking journalists on tours of the lava fields and active volcanoes of Iceland's dramatic landscape. When her friends started suggesting that she should run for leader, Vigdís wasn't sure. She didn't know if she was the right person.

One day, Vigdís got a letter from the entire crew of a fishing trip. They told her they understood that women had been undervalued for too long and they wanted her to become their president. Vigdís decided to try.

After being elected, Vigdís realized how important her victory was. By being elected to the most visible position of power in her country, she let other women know that there was nothing they weren't capable of doing. From her new position she set about working for trees to be planted, education to be strengthened, and the rights of women to be taken seriously. Vigdís once said:

"THE GREATEST JOY IN LIFE IS BEING ALIVE— IF YOU CAN HANDLE LIFE, THAT IS. THIS MEANS OFFERING THE BEST OF YOURSELF TO SOCIETY: YOUR HONESTY, AMBITION, MIND, AND LOVE FOR PEOPLE. BEING CURIOUS AND WANTING TO USE YOUR EYES AND EARS WILL MAKE YOU WHAT YOU ARE."

Vigdís would lead her country for sixteen years. In that time, she dedicated herself to helping as many people as she could. Once a week, she would leave the door to her office open so that anyone could come in and tell her their problems, no matter how big or small.

As a result of the way that Vigdís and other Icelanders went about creating the kind of world they want to live in, their country is now ranked as the number-one place in the world to be a woman.

ANNE FRANK

(1929–1945)

For two years, Anne lived with her family in a secret annex, hidden behind a bookcase. The Nazis had occupied her home town of Amsterdam and were rounding up Jewish people, then taking them to concentration camps to be killed.

Anne and her family had to whisper when they spoke, walk barefoot, and try not to flush the toilet in the day, to prevent the people in the business below from hearing them. Anne spent a lot of her time writing in her diary, which she called Kitty. It had been a present for her thirteenth birthday and was a book meant for autographs, bound in red and white cloth.

In her diary, Anne wrote about the way the Jews had been treated in Amsterdam, her relationship with her father, and even her first kiss with a boy called Peter, who was part of another Jewish family who moved into the secret annex.

Despite the horrors that were going on around her, and the tragic circumstances in which she was forced to live, Anne wrote:

"'AS LONG AS THIS EXISTS,' I THOUGHT, 'AND I MAY LIVE TO SEE IT, THIS SUNSHINE, THE CLOUDLESS SKIES, WHILE THIS LASTS, I CANNOT BE UNHAPPY.' THE BEST REMEDY FOR THOSE WHO ARE AFRAID, LONELY OR UNHAPPY IS TO GO OUTSIDE ..."

Through all the pain and fear that Anne had to live in, she always found comfort in nature. She would spend hours staring out of a small window at a chestnut tree that stood outside the house. The tree gave her hope.

Tragically, Anne's family were eventually discovered and sent away to a concentration camp. Although Anne was killed, her father survived, and he fulfilled his daughter's dream of becoming a writer by helping to get her diary published. It has since become known around the world as a powerful work by a thoughtful, brave, joyful young girl. Anne's diary is proof that there are people who can keep hope burning even when it might feel as though all is lost.

ANURUDH GANESAN

(BORN 2000)

When Anurudh was just six months old, his grandparents carried him ten miles across India to get vaccinated against polio, a deadly, infectious disease that can leave people permanently weak, especially in the legs. It was a journey that could only be made by foot. By the time the family arrived at the vaccination station, they were told the vaccine had become useless. It had needed to be kept at a low temperature and there was no way of doing so in their remote region of India.

What happened to Anurudh is a very common problem. Many people across the world live in remote, inhospitable areas that can only be accessed by foot, bicycle, or pack animals like donkeys or camels. When vaccines are transported that way, it's almost impossible to keep them cool enough to stay effective.

One day, at the dinner table, Anurudh's parents told him about the journey his grandparents had taken him on when he was a baby. Anurudh then learned that every year, over 1.5 million children die from illnesses that could be prevented by vaccines. He set out to help.

Anurudh took apart a fridge to see how it managed to keep things cool. He then built his own cooling system, one that wouldn't need electricity or ice to run. He called his invention the VAXXWAGON. It's a device that is attached to a bicycle and transforms some of the energy produced by pedaling into energy that can keep vaccines cool. It enables people

to safely transport medicines to places that are difficult to reach.

At the age of just fifteen, Anurudh won an award at the Google Science Fair. It was the perfect place for him to show-case the VAXXWAGON, because Anurudh believes that:

"SCIENCE ALLOWS ME TO DREAM, IMAGINE, EXPLORE, AND QUESTION UNKNOWN THINGS. THIS CREATIVE FREEDOM ALLOWS ME TO BE LIMITLESS IN MY THINKING!"

As Anurudh discovered, it doesn't matter whether you're a professor with expensive equipment or a boy with an old fridge, science is about using your mind to come up with incredible solutions for the most important problems of our time.

DAME EVELYN GLENNIE

(BORN 1965)

Evelyn grew up on a farm in Scotland and learned to play piano from the age of eight. As she grew older, she started to lose her hearing. Evelyn was deaf by the time she turned twelve. That was when she started being drawn to percussion instruments. With drums, shakers, and cymbals, Evelyn found she could sense the vibrations they created. It didn't matter that she couldn't hear the music with her ears, because she could feel it with her body.

At sixteen, Evelyn was offered a place to study percussion at the Royal Academy of Music. She played barefoot so that she could feel the vibrations through her feet. Her talent was undeniable. Evelyn won many awards and gave numerous stirring performances, both alone and with orchestras.

She's now regarded as one of the greatest percussionists in the world. She has performed in over forty countries, starred in multiple documentaries, written and recorded her own work, and had numerous pieces of music written just for her. Evelyn once said:

"I DO KNOW THAT WE CAN ALL FEEL LIMITED. WE CAN FEEL SLIGHTLY DOUBTFUL OF OURSELVES, EVEN IN MUSICAL SITUATIONS. I'VE BEEN IN THIS INDUSTRY FOR SO MANY YEARS BUT I HAVE DOUBTS SOMETIMES. IT'S JUST TAKING THAT FIRST STEP. AS A MUSICIAN, IF I'M CONTRACTED TO LEARN A PIECE OF MUSIC, I BEGIN BY JUST LOOKING AT THE FIRST PHRASE OR THE FIRST BAR. EVEN IF IT TAKES HALF AN HOUR, YOU CAN BUILD FROM THAT FIRST STEP. IT'S THE PERSISTENCE AND THE REALIZATION THAT YOU CAN HANDLE IT IN BITE-SIZE BITS."

There are many tasks that appear incredibly daunting at first, whether it's learning a piece of music, starting a big homework project, or heading out on a long journey. But none of those tasks are meant to be done in one giant leap. Each is completed by making a number of small steps, one after the other. As Evelyn discovered, if we take things bit by bit, even big challenges become manageable, and we find ourselves capable of doing the most incredible things.

SELENA GOMEZ

(BORN 1992)

Selena was raised by her mother, who worked three jobs and still found time to act in plays at the theater. Selena was bitten by the acting bug too. At the age of ten, she got a part in the kid's TV show *Barney & Friends*. From there, she went on to act in shows like the *Wizards of Waverly Place*, and release hit songs like "Good for You" and "Same Old Love."

But even though her career was going well, it didn't mean that life was easy. Selena suffered from a disease called lupus, which meant her immune system would sometimes start to attack healthy parts of her body for no reason. She also struggled with mental health problems, like anxiety and depression. These were caused partly by all the hurtful, intrusive things that journalists and a few unkind people on the internet would say about her.

Selena decided that she would be open about how she felt. That way, lots of the young people who looked up to her could feel like it was okay to be open about how they felt too.

In one speech against bullying, Selena told her fans:

∿∿∿∿∿∿∿∿∿∿∿∿∿∿

"YOU ARE NOT DEFINED BY AN INSTAGRAM PHOTO, BY A LIKE, BY A COMMENT—

THAT DOES NOT DEFINE YOU. I WANT YOU GUYS TO KNOW THAT THE TRICK IS TO FOCUS ON THE LOVE. AND WHAT I WANT YOU GUYS TO DO, EVERY RUDE COMMENT THAT YOU GET, EVERY PERSON THAT TRIES TO HURT YOU, PERSONALLY OR THROUGH THE INTERNET, I WANT YOU TO FORGIVE THEM. JUST FORGIVE THEM. 'CAUSE THEY DON'T EVEN KNOW."

∿∿∿∿∿∿∿∿∿∿∿∿∿∿

Early on in her career, Selena realized that it didn't matter what a few spiteful people said about her. What mattered was that she had the love of her mom, her friends, and her fans. She knew that the people who try to hurt us are almost always people who have been hurt themselves. If we can learn to forgive them, we become free to be who we really are.

YASH GUPTA

(BORN 1996)

When he was fourteen, Yash broke his glasses while practicing taekwondo. He had to spend an entire week without being able to see properly. It was incredibly difficult. Without his full sight, Yash struggled to learn anything at his California middle school that week.

After carrying out some research, Yash was shocked to discover that there were around thirteen million kids around the world who needed glasses but couldn't afford them. A week had been hard enough, but it was tough to imagine how it might feel to spend your whole life without being able to see.

Yash decided to do something about it. Despite his age, he started an organization called Sight Learning, which aimed to provide glasses for kids in countries where they were difficult to get hold of.

Over the following years, Yash would devote as much time and energy as he could to growing Sight Learning. He built a website, handed out fliers, knocked on doors, and even tutored kids younger than him to raise money.

Sight Learning has since donated over one million dollars' worth of glasses to kids in America, India, Honduras, Mexico, and Haiti. Students from other schools have even started their own chapters of Sight Learning. According to Yash:

"KIDS ARE PASSIONATE AND CAN MAKE A DIFFERENCE. IT'S JUST A MATTER OF FINDING OUT WHAT YOU CARE ABOUT AND FOCUSING ON THAT."

Everyone finds a different route to their passion. When Yash broke his glasses, there was no way he could have predicted it would set him on a path to helping so many children around the world. He proved that if we keep our eyes and ears open, we might be surprised by the causes that call out to us. There are so many ways of making a difference; it's just up to you to find your own.

EDWARD EVERETT HALE

(1822–1909)

School bored Edward senseless. He was used to being allowed to follow his own passions and curiosities: growing up, Edward was surrounded by a loving family who encouraged him to invent his own games and concoct his own experiments.

To make school more exciting, Edward read all the novels he could get his hands on, started an astronomy club, and tried to learn the art of photography at a time when it had barely even begun. His parents were always supportive of his unusual passions, even if they confused his teachers.

After leaving school, Edward traveled around America, eventually settling down as the pastor of a church in Worcester, Massachusetts. He helped Irish immigrants who had left their country due to the potato famine, fought for the freedom of enslaved black people, and called for education to be made available to everyone.

Edward also wrote a lot of stories, many of which were funny and moving. One called *Ten Times One is Ten* became very famous. In the story, a group of men meet at the funeral of their friend and talk about all the amazing ways he changed their lives for the better. In his honor, they decide to form a club with the motto:

"LOOK UP AND NOT DOWN;
LOOK FORWARD AND NOT BACK;
LOOK OUT AND NOT IN;
LEND A HAND."

The idea was so powerful that it prompted some readers to start their own real-life Lend a Hand club. Soon, there were clubs all over the world, dedicated to helping anyone who needed their assistance.

The Lend a Hand Society still exists today. Its aim remains the same: to offer the entire world the love and care that Edward was shown growing up. Edward believed that we are all brothers and sisters, so we should do everything we can to look after each other like family.

MILADA HORÁKOVÁ

(1901–1950)

During the First World War, Milada was kicked out of school for taking part in an anti-war protest. She would spend the rest of her life standing up for what she thought was right, even when it meant putting herself in grave danger.

After the Nazis came to power in Germany, Hitler decided to invade and occupy Milada's home country, Czechoslovakia. Milada formed a secret network of women's resistance groups to fight back. The Nazis eventually uncovered them and Milada was sent to a concentration camp in Germany where she spent many months in solitary confinement.

When American troops rolled into Bavaria, Milada was finally freed. She returned to Prague and joined the political party that she hoped would benefit her people most. Then the communists took power and started arresting anyone who dared to speak out against them. This included Milada. She had spoken up about how they falsely accused people of things just so they could execute them or lock them away. The communist regime arrested Milada too and sentenced her to death.

In one of the last letters she wrote to her daughter, Jana, Milada said:

"LEARN FROM EVERYBODY, NO MATTER HOW UNIMPORTANT! GO THROUGH THE WORLD WITH OPEN EYES, AND LISTEN NOT ONLY TO YOUR OWN PAINS AND INTERESTS, BUT ALSO TO THE PAINS, INTERESTS AND LONGINGS OF OTHERS . . . MAN DOESN'T LIVE IN THE WORLD ALONE; IN THAT THERE IS GREAT HAPPINESS, BUT ALSO A TREMENDOUS RESPONSIBILITY."

From her years as a schoolgirl to her years as a resistance leader, Milada always stayed true to her beliefs. She spent her life listening to the pains of others and doing everything she could to help them.

MOLLIE HUGHES

(BORN 1990)

The temperature sunk to minus forty-five and powerful winds swept across the barren ground. Dense blizzards called whiteouts made it nearly impossible to see. Still, Mollie kept going. After nearly sixty days, she became the youngest woman ever to ski alone from the edge of Antarctica to the South Pole. It was an incredibly dangerous and difficult journey. In other words, it was exactly the kind of challenge Mollie loved.

When she was seventeen, Mollie left England on a school trip to Africa and climbed the steep, rocky slopes of Mount Kenya. She knew then these were the kind of adventures she wanted to spend her life having. She went to university to study sports biology and decided she wanted to climb Mount Everest, the tallest mountain above sea level in the world.

Despite our advances in technology, climbing Everest is still far from safe. Eleven people died in 2019 while trying to get up the mountain. But that didn't stop Mollie. Neither did climbing across deep crevasses on rickety ladders, running from avalanches, or opening her bottle to find the water inside it had frozen. At twenty-six, she became the youngest woman ever to climb the mountain from both sides.

Her advice to anyone who wants to follow in her footsteps is that:

"YOU NEED TO CONVINCE YOURSELF THAT YOU CAN AND VISUALIZE YOURSELF SUCCEEDING. FOCUS ON SUCCEEDING IN SOMETHING YOU LOVE AND ARE PASSIONATE ABOUT. IF YOUR AMBITION MEANS EVERYTHING TO YOU, WORK WILL NEVER FEEL LIKE WORK, YOU WILL BE UNWAVERINGLY COMMITTED AND MOST LIKELY SUCCEED."

If she hadn't had such a passion for embarking on perilous expeditions, there's no way Mollie would have been able to overcome all the challenges she faced along the way. She knows that the things we can do best are the things we truly care about. If it's something you want more than anything, you'll find a way to get up that mountain, no matter what.

GERTRUDE JEKYLL

(1843–1932)

Gertrude was five when her family moved out of the chaotic city of London to a house in the countryside of Surrey. She would spend hours out in the garden, getting to know the plants and flowers.

At eighteen, she went to university to study art. It was there that she met other artists, like John Ruskin, and studied the paintings of J. M. W. Turner, who used golden yellows and otherworldly blues to conjure emotional landscapes. She became well known as an artist who could capture the spirit of the natural world.

When her father died, Gertrude moved with her family back to the country house in Surrey where she'd grown up. She set about redesigning the garden. Gertrude made use of traditional roses, lavender, and hostas, but she set them out in unusual ways, around water features and in bright borders. Every texture, color, and arrangement was carefully chosen, so that her garden grew to become a piece of art.

Gertrude's eyesight got worse as she got older and she found it more and more difficult to paint. Instead, she devoted herself to gardening. She traveled across the Mediterranean with friends, collecting plants and sending them back to England. Gertrude was painting with flowers, using cold blues and whites, then hot pinks and yellows, to bring surprise and wonder to the gardens that people asked her to design. And what did she learn?

> "THE LESSON I HAVE THOROUGHLY LEARNED, AND WISH TO PASS ON TO OTHERS, IS TO KNOW THE ENDURING HAPPINESS THAT THE LOVE OF A GARDEN GIVES."

Gertrude's advice has even been backed up by scientific research. Studies have shown that spending time out in nature can make us feel happier and healthier. It turns out that what Gertrude discovered for herself at the age of five is something we could all benefit from.

During the course of her life, Gertrude designed over 300 gardens. Now, some of the gardens created by Gertrude attract thousands of visitors every year. There's even a flower named after her, a vivid pink rose that blooms early every year.

MATINA KATSIVELI

(BORN 1954)

In recent years, hundreds of thousands of people have made the treacherous journey across the Mediterranean Sea in search of somewhere safe to live. These people are often fleeing violence and persecution in countries like Syria, Afghanistan, and Iran.

Many of the refugees travel in dangerously overloaded, flimsy boats that might sink in the middle of the sea, far from help. If they manage to make the crossing, people often arrive on the shores of Greek islands. One of these islands is called Leros and it's Matina's home.

When refugees first began arriving on Leros, Matina became determined to help. For people who've had to flee their homes, who've lost family members, and who have no idea what the future will hold in store for them, Matina realized how much it can mean to have someone waiting to welcome you.

Despite not having any support from governments or institutions, Matina and other volunteers spent their own money to make sure the people who arrived on their island had fresh clothes, toiletries, and food. They formed a group called Leros Solidarity Network. The group managed to raise enough money to convert an old house on the island into somewhere that the refugees who arrived could stay. Matina believes that:

ᴧᴧᴧᴧᴧᴧᴧᴧᴧᴧᴧᴧᴧᴧᴧᴧᴧᴧᴧᴧᴧᴧ

"THE STORIES OF THE PEOPLE WHO WE HELPED AND CONNECTED WITH ARE OUR GOLD, WHICH NO ONE CAN TAKE AWAY FROM US. AND AS I ALWAYS LIKE TO SAY, EVEN TO HELP ONE PERSON IS A VERY BIG DEAL."

ᴧᴧᴧᴧᴧᴧᴧᴧᴧᴧᴧᴧᴧᴧᴧᴧᴧᴧᴧᴧᴧᴧ

For many people who are forced to leave their countries as refugees, life can become a constant fight to find somewhere they're accepted. We all need help at certain times in our lives and we are all put in positions where we can help others too. As Matina said, even to help one person can make a world of difference.

HELEN KELLER

(1880–1968)

At the age of just one and a half, Helen became both deaf and blind. It was the result of an illness that we now believe to have been either scarlet fever or rubella. Her condition left Helen frustrated and, as she grew up, this frustration often turned into anger. Everyone could see that she was smart, but it was a struggle to find ways that she could show her intelligence.

One day, Helen's parents found a new teacher, Anne, for their daughter. Anne had also had some problems with her eyesight, so she could understand a little of what Helen was going through, but it was still incredibly difficult to teach words to someone who could neither hear nor see. They made a huge step forward when Anne realized one day she could run water over one of Helen's hands while spelling out the sign-language word for water on her other hand.

With Anne's help, Helen learned not only how to communicate in sign language and to read Braille, but how to speak with her mouth too. She used her newfound voice to share her ideas with the world. She spoke out for the rights of disabled people, women, workers, and the poor. She became well known for her powerful, intelligent speeches and writing.

Helen and Anne went on many tours together, speaking to audiences around the world. At the end of each appearance, the audience were invited to ask questions. In one, Helen was asked if she wanted her sight back more than anything. She replied:

"NO! NO! I WOULD RATHER WALK WITH A FRIEND IN THE DARK THAN ALONE IN THE LIGHT."

Helen knew that the most important part of life was not her body, her abilities, or her limitations; it was the people she had around her. As Helen pointed out, it is often not our circumstances that matter, but who we're in our circumstances with. Even the most difficult and trying times can be made bearable with a friend, and similarly, even the most wonderful, exciting, extravagant moment might not feel like much at all if you don't have anyone to share it with.

WANDA LANDOWSKA

(1879–1959)

Before there were pianos, there were harpsichords. Harpsichords are believed to have been invented all the way back in the medieval ages. Although they might look like pianos, they have an almost twinkly sound and often feature two keyboards, one above the other.

Wanda started out playing the piano when she was just four. Her teachers quickly saw that she had a gift. Wanda wasn't drawn to modern music. The kind of music that interested her was older, coming from the fifteenth and sixteenth centuries: the age of the harpsichord.

When she got older, Wanda traveled around museums and libraries, learning all she could about early music and how it was played. She fell in love with the harpsichord and started playing it more than the piano. She dreamed of playing old pieces of music how they would originally have been heard, hundreds of years before her time.

On February 21, 1942, Wanda played one of the most famous pieces of classical music for a packed crowd in New York's Town Hall. It was the first time that century that Bach's "Goldberg Variations" had been played in public on the instrument it was written for: the harpsichord.

Someone once asked Wanda about practicing. She told them:

"I NEVER PRACTICE, I ALWAYS PLAY."

In those few words, Wanda revealed something really powerful. What's the difference, after all, between practicing and playing? Practice sounds like a chore and something you have to get through before you can get to the good part. Playing, on the other hand, sounds joyful. Wanda realized she could enjoy the act of practicing so much that it became as exciting and fulfilling as playing. It was just a matter of how she chose to think about things.

In 1925, Wanda set up a school near Paris dedicated to the kind of early music she'd fallen in love with as a child. She didn't want the students there to practice; she wanted them to play.

JONAH LARSON

(BORN 2008)

At the age of five, Jonah learned how to crochet. He'd found an old crochet hook in a box of craft material and used a YouTube tutorial to learn how to make a dishcloth out of yarn. As a boy who'd struggled to behave in school because his mind was always racing, Jonah found crocheting really calmed him down. He focused on stitches and rows, gradually creating more and more complex pieces.

His behavior improved and he got even better at crocheting too. Jonah was seven when he created a blanket made out of 800 different flowers stitched together. By the time he was twelve, he could crochet a hat in just thirty minutes. Jonah became so good that he could create beautiful pieces of clothing without even having to look down at his hands. Instead, he'd watch history documentaries while he wove his designs.

Jonah decided to use his incredible talent to help others. When he was a baby, Jonah had been adopted from a village in Ethiopia by his American parents. He decided he wanted to use his crocheting to raise money for the kids back in the village he'd been born in.

By publishing books, posting videos, selling his creations, and asking for donations, Jonah managed to raise enough money to build a library and a science center in his village in Ethiopia. He realized that if he hadn't been adopted, the children in that village would have been his classmates. He wanted them to have access to books and science equipment, just like he had.

Jonah's advice for other kids is:

"DO WHAT YOU LOVE AND DON'T CARE WHAT OTHER PEOPLE THINK."

It turned out that what Jonah loved was crocheting. Although it may have been an unusual hobby for a boy of his age, he didn't care what anyone else thought. Crocheting made him happy and it turned out to be a superpower he could use to make the world a better place.

RITA LEVI-MONTALCINI
(1909–2012)

During the Second World War, Rita would bicycle around the countryside near her home in Turin, Italy, searching for eggs. The eggs weren't for eating. Rita was using them to conduct scientific research in her bedroom. She wanted to discover more about what went on as mammals grow from a few cells into complex creatures.

At the time, Jewish people like Rita were being persecuted across Europe. She had left her position at the University of Turin because she didn't want to get the other scientists in trouble for working with someone who was Jewish.

But Rita knew how important her work was and she was determined to pursue it no matter what. When bombs were falling around her house, she would take her microscope down to the basement and continue her investigations into how it was possible for such simple cells to become such complicated animals.

Near the end of the war, Rita went to work as a nurse, helping sick and wounded soldiers. She saw it all as part of the same thing: looking for ways that she could help others.

Rita once explained that:

"I TELL YOUNG PEOPLE: DO NOT THINK OF YOURSELF, THINK OF OTHERS. THINK OF THE FUTURE THAT AWAITS YOU, THINK ABOUT WHAT YOU CAN DO AND DO NOT FEAR ANYTHING."

After the war, Rita was invited to Washington University in America to continue her studies. For her work, she was awarded the Nobel Prize, the highest honor in science. By continuing her quest for knowledge, even during the hardest, darkest times of her life, Rita managed to push our scientific understanding forward and improve the lives of the millions of people who benefited from her discoveries.

DOROTHY LEVITT

(1882–1922)

Newspapers called her "the fastest girl on earth" after she hurtled through the Brighton Speed Trials at almost eighty miles per hour. It was 1905 and Dorothy had set the new ladies' land speed record. The car she was driving was a Napier.

Dorothy had first started working at Napier as a typist and secretary. After she struck up a friendship with one of the bosses, he realized that there was something special about Dorothy. She convinced him to have someone teach her how to drive.

Dorothy was soon competing in many different races and breaking multiple records. She won a hill climb in France, came second in a speed trial along the Bexhill seafront in England, and came fourth in a German race that was around 1,200 miles long. Dorothy would always compete in the races with her small black dog, Dodo, sitting at her side.

But despite her achievements, many men were still dismissive about female drivers. Some tracks refused to let Dorothy compete. At the time, certain people didn't think it was right for ladies to drive at all, let alone take part in races. British women were not even allowed to vote in elections until 1928 because they weren't believed to be as rational as men. In a guide she wrote for female drivers, Dorothy explained:

"I AM CONSTANTLY ASKED BY SOME ASTONISHED PEOPLE 'DO YOU REALLY UNDERSTAND ALL THE HORRID MACHINERY OF A MOTOR, AND COULD YOU MEND IT IF IT BROKE DOWN?' ... THE DETAILS OF AN ENGINE MAY SOUND COMPLICATED AND LOOK 'HORRID,' BUT AN ENGINE IS EASILY MASTERED."

As Dorothy found out, there will always be people who find it difficult to make sense of those who don't conform to their expectations. She didn't care. She loved driving at spine-tingling speeds, regardless of whether it was considered ladylike. In the end, the biggest obstacle Dorothy had to overcome wasn't understanding the engine of her own car; it was getting past the people who told her she couldn't do the thing she loved, simply because she was a woman.

SOL LEWITT

(1928–2007)

Sol believed that anyone could be an artist. When he was putting together his shows, he would get lots of people involved in the painting. He didn't believe art was about the talent of a painter, but about powerful ideas and how they can bring us together. Many of his works were simple instructions written on paper that could be used to recreate his artworks again and again, by anyone who wanted to try them.

Sol had been painting ever since he was a boy and his mom took him along to art lessons at a museum called the Wadsworth Atheneum in Hartford, Conneticut. The two of them had moved in with Sol's aunt because his father had died. He used to draw on scraps of wrapping paper from the supply store his aunt owned.

As he grew older, Sol played with simple colors and shapes to create white cubes, bold patterns, and vibrant splashes of paint. He scribbled on walls. He built huge sculptures. In all of his work, he reduced his creations to the simplest forms and lines. This new style of art came to be known as minimalism.

Although many people found Sol's artwork entrancing, there were a number of critics who didn't understand it. They thought the work was so simple

that it was lazy and meaningless. Sol didn't care. In a letter to an artist called Eva Hesse, he wrote:

"YOU BELONG IN THE MOST SECRET PART OF YOU. DON'T WORRY ABOUT COOL, MAKE YOUR OWN UNCOOL. MAKE YOUR OWN, YOUR OWN WORLD. IF YOU FEAR, MAKE IT WORK FOR YOU—DRAW AND PAINT YOUR FEAR AND ANXIETY."

As Sol had come to understand, art isn't about making something cool or perfect or clever. It's about finding ways of expressing our thoughts, feelings, and ideas. It's about building our own worlds and inviting other people in to visit them.

JOHANNES LICHTENAUER
(FOURTEENTH CENTURY)

In the fourteenth century, knowing how to use a sword could mean the difference between life and death. You might be robbed by bandits while traveling between towns. You might be called up to fight for your king. And you might be forced to protect your home from marauding soldiers. The outcome of each of these situations depended on your skill with a weapon, most likely a sword.

Johannes was a German master in the art of sword fighting. He traveled all around Europe, learning everything he could about the different tricks and techniques for armed combat. He then put together what he'd learned into a series of teachings. Johannes placed an emphasis on not trying to look flashy or fancy, but striking directly.

His teachings would found the Lichtenauer School of Swordsmanship, a series of lessons that would shape German fighting techniques for hundreds of years to come. As Johannes never wrote anything down himself, it was up to his students to record what he said. They often did this in the form of poems. In one, Johannes told them:

"AVOID FOOLHARDINESS, DO NOT ATTEMPT TO MATCH FOUR OR SIX OPPONENTS AT ONCE.

RESTRAIN YOUR AMBITION, THIS WILL BENEFIT YOU. HE IS A COURAGEOUS MAN WHO CAN STAND AGAINST HIS EQUAL, WHILE IT IS NO SHAME TO FLEE FROM FOUR OR SIX."

During the time in which Johannes lived, it was unfortunately almost impossible to avoid violence. We now know that there are much better ways of solving problems and living alongside each other than fighting, but that doesn't mean we don't have anything to learn from the Lichtenauer School. Whether you're a medieval knight with a sword, a mathematician faced with a difficult equation, or a kid in a playground, there's never any shame in admitting defeat. There will always be things we can do and there will always be things we can't do; it's just a matter of deciding which is which.

GRAÇA MACHEL
(BORN 1945)

Graça was born in Mozambique, the eldest of six siblings. Her father died just weeks before she came into the world. Before he passed away, he made his wife promise that, no matter what, she would make sure Graça received an education. It wouldn't be easy. Graça's family were poor and the majority of children in Mozambique at the time didn't get any schooling at all.

But Graça managed to get a scholarship to a school in Maputo, the capital of Mozambique. At the time, the country was still occupied by Portugal, who had invaded many centuries earlier. When Graça started at the school, she was shocked and confused to find that she was the only black student in a class of white kids whose ancestors were from Portugal.

Graça would spend the next years of her life fighting to free her country from the Portuguese. Once this had been achieved, she looked for other ways she could help her fellow humans. Graça once said that everyone should:

"ASK YOURSELF WHAT YOU CAN DO TO MAKE A DIFFERENCE. AND THEN TAKE THAT ACTION, NO MATTER HOW LARGE OR HOW SMALL"

It's clear that Graça believed her own words. When she took on the post of Minister for Education for Mozambique, there were only 400,000 children in school. By the time she left, 1.5 million kids were getting an education. Graça knew how important learning had been in her life and was determined to give other kids from her country the same opportunity.

Graça has since dedicated her life to fighting for the rights of those who need support. She has helped children whose lives have been torn apart by war, refugees who have nowhere safe to call home, and women who have been denied the rights that every human being deserves.

Graça has spent her time doing what she has told all of us to do: looking for the ways in which we can help others. There is no cause too small and no problem so large that you should give up on it. We can all make a difference, just like Graça.

NICOLE MAINES

(BORN 1997)

By day, she's an investigative reporter called Nia Nal. By night, she's a superhero called Dreamer. Nicole's character in *Supergirl* has superhuman strength and the ability to see into the future through her dreams; she uses her powers to protect those who need help. She's also the first transgender superhero on TV.

Nicole had realized from an early age that she didn't feel comfortable in her body. Although she'd been given a boy's name and a boy's body, she felt inside that she was a girl. So she chose a girl's name for herself and started living her life as a female.

Kids at Nicole's school bullied her, calling her "it" and following her into the bathroom. She would go home crying, thinking that there was something wrong with her. In response, the school assigned an adult to stay by her side at all times. That only made her feel even more cut off from everyone else.

But Nicole refused to stop fighting for who she was. When a law was going to be passed in their home state of Maine that stopped transgender people using the bathrooms they wanted to, Nicole stood up in the state capitol and explained what it meant to her to be able to go into a bathroom where she felt safe. The law wasn't passed. After meeting Nicole and hearing about her life, the politicians could understand why the rights of transgender people needed to be protected.

When asked for advice to a young person who thinks they might be transgender, Nicole said:

- -

"DON'T RUSH YOURSELF. I DON'T EVER WANT SOMEONE TO FEEL LIKE THEY'RE WRONG FOR CHOOSING NOT TO COME OUT, OR FOR COMING OUT AND HAVING PEOPLE NOT ACCEPT THEM. YOUR IDENTITY IS ENTIRELY YOURS AND YOU OWE IT TO NOBODY."

- -

Nicole is proud of being the first transgender superhero because it means she can be a role model to other kids who are going through what she went through. If anyone's ever made to feel ashamed of who they are, Dreamer will be there to remind them that they're not alone.

SPYRIDON MARINATOS

(1901–1974)

The Minoan civilization began on the Greek island of Crete around 5,000 years ago. Its people built grand, four-story palaces, painted detailed frescoes, and crafted elaborate pieces of pottery. Their powerful fleet of ships soon saw their influence spread across the Mediterranean. Then, around 1500 BC, their civilization mysteriously collapsed. Historians still aren't entirely sure why.

Spyridon is an archaeologist from Greece. For many years, he looked after the Heraklion Museum on Crete, where many of the treasures recovered from the ancient Minoans are kept.

When Spyridon left the museum, he traveled to various Aegean islands, running digs to unearth the artifacts left behind from ancient civilizations. He soon came up with an idea: perhaps the Minoans had been wiped out by a natural disaster. Perhaps a volcanic eruption had caused a tsunami, both of which might have devastated the islands the Minoans called home.

On the island of Thera, under layers of volcanic stone called pumice, Spyridon uncovered the remains of an ancient city called Akrotiri. He was sixty-six and would spend the next seven years of his life unearthing the streets, walls, and artworks of a civilization that hadn't been seen for thousands of years. Every new discovery thrilled Spyridon, who knew that:

"THE MORE YOU KNOW, THE MORE YOU UNDERSTAND. I HAVE DONE THIS JOB FOR FIFTY YEARS, AND I TRY TO PERFECT MYSELF IN ORDER TO DETECT MORE. ONCE A YEAR I REREAD HOMER. EACH TIME I SEE THE TEXT WITH NEW EYES. HOMER IS THE SAME, OF COURSE, BUT I HAVE CHANGED."

What Spyridon knew is that as we grow, we change, and as we change, we begin to see the world differently. If we can leave ourselves open to new ideas, thoughts, and possibilities, then we'll be amazed by the things we discover. It might be a new way of seeing something, it might be a new way of understanding someone, or it might even be an ancient city, found again after thousands of years.

AISA MIJENO

While volunteering in the Kalinga region of the Philippines, Aisa met many people who have to walk six hours every two days just to get kerosene for their lamps and cookers. These people live in remote areas with no public transport and rely on gas for light. As the country is spread across many islands, it is difficult to connect all homes to a power grid.

Aisa wondered if there might be a way of helping those who live off the grid. As a scientist, she believes it's important to:

"HAVE THE INITIATIVE TO FIND ANSWERS TO YOUR QUESTIONS EVEN WITHOUT EXPECTING SOMETHING TANGIBLE IN RETURN. I AM PRETTY CERTAIN THAT ALL OF US HAVE LOTS OF QUESTIONS IN OUR MINDS; MOST OF US JUST TEND TO DISMISS THEM BECAUSE WE ARE NOT THAT MOTIVATED TO SOLVE IT. EVEN WITHOUT ANY SORT OF REWARD, YOU SHOULD CONTINUOUSLY QUEST FOR ANSWERS."

And that's exactly what Aisa did. She joined Batangas State University so she could begin her research and eventually came up with a solution to the problem she'd been considering: a lamp that could be powered by the most common resource on planet earth—saltwater.

The "SALt lamp" works by submerging two different metals in the water, creating electricity. All it needs to run is saltwater and a small part that needs to be changed once every six months. Two tablespoons of salt and one glass of water is enough to keep the lamp shining for eight hours. For many people, it means no longer having to make long, difficult journeys to distant towns. All they need to do is fill their lamps with water from the ocean.

Over 1,500 communities across the Philippines now rely on Aisa's invention. She went looking for an answer and she found one, helping thousands of people by doing so.

NUJEEN MUSTAFA

(BORN 1999)

Since the beginning of the Syrian civil war in 2011, over five million Syrians have fled the country in search of somewhere safe to live. It's a huge number and behind each one is the personal story of someone who has lost their home.

Nujeen's journey out of Syria may have been even more difficult than most. Born with cerebral palsy, Nujeen couldn't walk, and so had spent most of her life in her family's fifth floor apartment. She had never been on a bus, a boat, or a train. She spent most of her time watching TV, which is how she taught herself to speak English.

When Nujeen's parents realized they would have to leave the country, they carried Nujeen down the stairs of their building. She would go on to cross eight countries in her wheelchair, as well as having to cross the sea in a tiny boat holding three times as many people as it was supposed to. It was a terrifying journey. Nujeen's older sister, Nisreen, pushed her the whole way. They had almost no money and some days all they had to eat was Nutella.

Nujeen eventually reached Germany, where she was reunited with her brother. She joined a school, wrote two books, and spoke out about the treatment of refugees around the world. Nujeen has said that:

> "EVERY CHILD NEEDS TO BELIEVE IN HIS OR HER ABILITIES. EVERY CHILD IS A SPECIAL PERSON. NO ONE COMES TO THIS WORLD JUST AS A NUMBER. EVERYONE HAS A ROLE TO PLAY AND AN IMPACT TO MAKE, HOWEVER LIMITED IN SIZE OR SCOPE."

Nujeen wants the world to understand that there are real human beings behind each statistic that you might hear reported on the news. And each of those human beings has something wonderful to offer the world. You do, I do, and Nujeen does. We are all capable of changing things for the better.

In Nujeen's honor, the stars of her favorite TV show recorded a scene in which they discussed the incredible girl who had traveled 3,400 miles in a wheelchair in search of somewhere new to call home.

MEI LIN NEO

(BORN 1987)

Giant clams are a species of mollusk that can be found in coral reefs around Asia, Indonesia, and the east coast of Africa. They grow to bigger than three feet across, weigh more than an adult lion, and live for over a hundred years. They're also in danger.

When Mei Lin first learned about the giant clams, she was looking for a research project to take on at university. She went for an interview to see whether she might be suitable and the professor asked if she had any experience with diving, marine biology, or giant clams. Mei Lin didn't. She explained that her biggest talent was probably arts and crafts, and that she'd once made a Hello Kitty doll that could turn its head 360 degrees. The professor decided to take a chance on her. She was accepted on to the project.

It wasn't a path Mei Lin had ever thought her life would take, but there's no way she'd change anything.

Since taking on the project, Mei Lin has spent years learning about the giant clams and studying them in their natural habitats. She's found herself trapped in reefs during storms, struggling to raise baby clams, and giving a TED Talk that has been watched by over a million people on YouTube.

The clams are endangered in the wild because many people harvest them for food and to use in aquariums. Mei Lin has made it her mission to try and protect them. Between 2011 and 2018, she led a huge project to raise baby clams and return them to the sea around Singapore.

The advice Mei Lin would give to any young person trying to plan for their future is:

> "DON'T BE AFRAID TO DREAM BIG! YOU NEVER KNOW WHERE YOUR DREAMS WILL TAKE YOU NEXT. AT LEAST, I KNOW MINE TOOK ME A LITTLE FURTHER THAN I HAD IMAGINED MYSELF..."

Mei Lin's dream is not just to help save her favorite marine animal, but to build up the relationship between people and their environment, and help everyone to understand just how important it is for us to look after the creatures we share our planet with.

NEZAHUALCOYOTL

(1402–1472)

If you look down at a Mexican hundred-peso note, you'll see Nezahualcoyotl's face staring back at you. Nezahualcoyotl was a prince and a poet who once wrote:

~~~~~~~~~~~~~~~~~~~~~~~~~~~~~

"STAND UP, BEAT YOUR DRUM GIVE OF YOURSELF, KNOW FRIENDSHIP."

~~~~~~~~~~~~~~~~~~~~~~~~~~~~~

Nezahualcoyotl's name means Hungry Coyote in the ancient language of the Acolhua people. Born a prince in 1402, in a place that is now known as Mexico, Hungry Coyote was destined to become the leader of his people.

The problem was that there were a number of other tribes living in Mesoamerica at that time and many of them were at war with each other. When a clan called the Tepanecs invaded Hungry Coyote's city, he was forced to flee and go into hiding. The Tepanecs had such a large and fierce army that resistance looked impossible.

For years, Hungry Coyote hid. He was caught, escaped from prison, lived in caves and huts, and disguised himself as a peasant. In all that time, however, his people never forgot him.

Hungry Coyote realized that the only way he would ever manage to return to his city would be by uniting the tribes of his land. By forming numerous alliances, he managed to raise an army of over 100,000 men and defeat the Tepanecs. Finally, in 1428, he could return home to the city where he was born.

With peace among the tribes, Hungry Coyote put all his energy into developing art, music, law, and science. He opened an academy of music that welcomed musicians from far and wide. He wrote poems that talked about his love of nature and his wonder at the universe. And he built beautiful hilltop gardens, featuring flowing water, dazzling collections of plants, and towering sculptures that illustrated the great Aztec myths.

Hungry Coyote had realized how much more could be achieved through friendship than through war. By uniting the people around him, he kickstarted a golden age of Aztec culture, and offered people the chance to live stable, happy lives.

FLORENCE NIGHTINGALE

(1820–1910)

As was normal for rich families at the time, Florence's parents expected her to get married at eighteen. Florence had other ideas.

"I can't get married," she said, "because I'm going to become a nurse."

Her parents weren't pleased but it was clear that there would be no changing Florence's mind. At the time, nursing was looked down on as a difficult, useless job. This was partly because hospitals at the time were not very advanced. They were dirty, cramped, and filled with disease. Quite often, if you went into a hospital, you'd only end up getting sicker.

Florence was determined to change that.

She trained at Pastor Theodor Fliedner's hospital in Germany, and then with the Sisters of Mercy in Paris. When she finally returned to England, Florence started hearing how awful the hospital conditions were for British soldiers fighting in the Crimean War. With thirty-seven other nurses, Florence set off to Turkey to try and help.

It was there that Florence got the nickname "the lady with the lamp" because the wounded soldiers would often see her peering in to check on them at night. Florence had realized the importance of keeping the hospitals clean, making sure the patients had enough to eat, and making them feel looked after. Thanks to Florence's revolutionary ideas, death rates in the camp hospitals fell from 40 percent to 2 percent. In a letter to a friend, she wrote:

"I ATTRIBUTE MY SUCCESS TO THIS: I NEVER GAVE NOR TOOK ANY EXCUSE."

An excuse, after all, is just a reason not to do something that you know can be done. It might be difficult, it might take a lot of strength, courage, and persistence, but it is possible. Florence knew that she could save lives with her nursing, by introducing new rules and making simple changes, like having the bed sheets washed and bandages changed regularly.

Florence's work helped to turn hospitals from dangerous, terrifying places, into spaces where patients were truly cared for. She refused to take excuses; the only thing she would accept was change.

HELENA NORBERG-HODGE

(BORN 1946)

Helena believes that giant companies are getting in the way of humans doing as well as they could. Rather than a world ruled by giant corporations, she thinks we would do better if everything was organized more locally. Instead of buying food shipped in from far away, we could buy food grown by farmers who live near us. And instead of buying clothes made on other continents, we could buy clothes made in our towns.

The problem is that by moving away from big companies, countries worry that they won't make as much money. Helena doesn't think this should be a problem. After all, why should countries measure how well they're doing by how much money they make, rather than by how happy the people living in them are?

Part of the reason Helena believes in doing things locally is because of a very remote region in India called Ladakh. Up until the 1970s, Ladakh was virtually cut off from the rest of the world by high mountains. When a road through the hills was built, people started arriving. Helena was one of those people. She watched as tourism, pollution, and money poured into the area. People became unwell and unhappy. They had never thought of themselves as poor, because they built their own houses and grew their own food, but now they struggled desperately to make money because they'd been told it was so important.

To anyone who wants to make a difference, Helena says:

"LISTEN TO WHAT REALLY MAKES YOUR HEART SING. WHERE WERE YOU AND WHAT WERE YOU DOING WHEN YOU EXPERIENCED MOMENTS OF DEEP CONTENTMENT AND HAPPINESS? LISTEN TO THE ANSWER AND USE IT AS A GUIDE."

Helena wants people to really consider which things make them happiest and then try to build a world around them. As many scientific studies have pointed out, it isn't a large amount of money that makes humans happier, but friends, and family, and strong communities. Helena believes it's time we started changing our world to reflect that.

DOLLY PARTON

(BORN 1946)

Dolly grew up with eleven brothers and sisters in a place called Locust Ridge, at the edge of Tennessee's Great Smoky Mountains. Her family were poor, which meant Dolly had to build her first guitar out of an old mandolin and two strings from a bass guitar.

Luckily, a lot of Dolly's family were musical too. Her uncle Billy played guitar and loved country music. He was one of the first people to really notice Dolly's talent. He gave Dolly her first proper guitar, managed to get her a spot on the radio, and helped her write some of her first songs. Uncle Billy became a leader for Dolly, and he helped prove to her what she was capable of. She would say that:

"IF YOUR ACTIONS CREATE A LEGACY THAT INSPIRES OTHERS TO DREAM MORE, LEARN MORE, DO MORE, AND BECOME MORE, THEN YOU ARE AN EXCELLENT LEADER."

Dolly would go on to become the best-loved country music star in history. She wrote hits like "I Will Always Love You," "Islands in the Stream," and "Jolene," and

acted in blockbuster films like *Steel Magnolias* and *Nine to Five*. Dolly even became so famous that she opened her own theme park, Dollywood, back in the smoky mountains where she grew up. It has rides based around the old traditions of Appalachia, like the Daredevil Falls, the Black Bear Trail, and the Tennessee Mountain Home.

Dolly wants to be a leader to young people, the same way that her uncle was once a leader to her. She knows that the people we look up to can shape our dreams, our thoughts, and our behavior. That's why she created Dolly Parton's Imagination Library, which sends books to poor children in America, the UK, Canada, Australia, and Ireland every month from the day they're born until the day they start kindergarten.

During the COVID pandemic, Dolly also donated a million dollars to help find a vaccine. She encouraged other people who could spare money to do the same. She knows how important it is to step up and set an example.

ITZHAK PERLMAN

(BORN 1945)

Many people would call Itzhak the greatest violinist alive today. His name is known far beyond the world of classical music. Itzhak has been on *Sesame Street*, played for royalty, and recorded the theme songs to famous films like *Schindler's List* and *Memoirs of a Geisha*. When he met Barack Obama, the former president told Itzhak that he listened to his playing whenever times got rough.

Itzhak had been through his share of rough times too. At the age of four, he contracted polio. He'd been born in Israel, which didn't have the most advanced medical facilities back in 1949. The disease left Itzhak with both legs paralyzed. From then on, he got around either on crutches or an electric scooter.

Itzhak was already playing violin. He'd heard a classical music performance and become set on learning to play the instrument. After a music school had turned him away at the age of three because they said he was too small to hold a violin properly, Itzhak started teaching himself how to play using a toy fiddle.

It paid off. A scout for an American talent show came to Israel and was blown away by Itzhak's playing. They flew him to New York and he performed on *The Ed Sullivan Show*. From that performance, Itzhak would go on to become hugely successful. His advice to anyone looking for their path in life is:

"THE KEY IS TO NEVER BE BORED. FIND SOMETHING THAT INTERESTS YOU IN PARTICULAR. IT'S A CHALLENGE, BUT YOU ALWAYS HAVE TO BE INTERESTED IN WHAT YOU DO— WHAT MAY BE ONE WAY TODAY MIGHT BECOME DIFFERENT TOMORROW. BE INVENTIVE. ASSESS YOURSELF. DO YOU LOVE MUSIC? DO YOU HAVE A PASSION? THE WORST THING IS TO FEEL THAT YOUR MUSIC IS A CHORE. DON'T GET CAUGHT THINKING YOU HAVE TO DO SOMETHING SPECIFIC, OR IN A SPECIFIC WAY. DO IT YOUR OWN WAY."

Itzhak was lucky enough to discover his passion for the violin at an incredibly young age. We don't all have to know what we want to do so early, but that doesn't mean we can't keep looking for the things that will light up our lives.

PLAUTUS

(254 BC–184 BC)

We don't know a lot about the life of Plautus for certain, although we are pretty sure he had thousands of ancient Romans howling with laughter in their huge cement theaters. That's why Plautus is often known as the father of Roman comedy.

It is believed that Plautus may have been born around 254 BC, in an Italian mountain village called Sarsina. His name means "flatfoot." Some say he became a Roman soldier and first came across the theater while serving in the army. Others say that he worked for many years as a carpenter in a theater, which is how he developed a love of plays. In one famous story about Plautus, he saved for many years to put on his plays, lost all his money, and was forced to work in a mill. They say he came up with the plot of his most popular story while grinding wheat.

Whatever the truth is about his life, we know that Plautus's many plays were hugely popular. They featured bathroom humor, silly characters, crazy plots, and exhilarating amounts of action.

One of Plautus's most famous plays was called *Pseudolus.* It told the story of a clever slave who formulates a plan to steal money from his master so that his friend can free the woman he loves. In the play, another slave called Harpax says:

"IF YOU SPEAK INSULTS YOU WILL HEAR THEM ALSO."

It's a simple piece of advice that makes perfect sense. If you say mean things about other people, you shouldn't be surprised if they say mean things back. Plautus knew that real comedy is something everyone can laugh at, rather than being cruel taunts directed at one person or group of people. He knew that humor has the power to unite us as human beings. When we laugh together, we come to realize all the things we have in common.

MARCO PONTES

(BORN 1963)

Marco grew up in a small village in the north of Brazil. His house was built of wood, on a street without pavement. Marco would play barefoot with his friends. Every weekend, he would bicycle out to the airport and watch the planes take off and land. He dreamed that one day he would be able to fly.

But getting a pilot's licence was expensive. Far too expensive for a boy like Marco. Instead, he realized that if he wanted to fly, he would have to join the air force. But even that would be difficult. Marco's friends laughed when they found out he was planning to become a pilot. They thought such jobs were only for rich kids and they told Marco he should give up his silly dreams.

He didn't listen. Marco studied two different courses in two different schools while also working as an electrician. Eventually he joined the air force and spent years as a safety officer, investigating accidents to work out what had gone wrong.

In 1998, Brazil held a search to find their very first astronaut. Marco was chosen out of thousands of candidates. It was clear that he was talented, experienced, and incredibly determined to achieve his dreams.

On March 30, 2006, Marco became the first Brazilian ever to go into space. He spent eight days on the International Space Station, performing experiments and checking everything was running smoothly. Marco had a lot of time to think while he was almost 250 miles from the surface of the earth. He realized that:

"PEOPLE ARE THE MOST IMPORTANT THINGS IN THIS LIFE. TREAT THEM AS SOMETHING PRECIOUS BECAUSE THAT IS EXACTLY WHAT THEY ARE. JUST LIKE OUR BEAUTIFUL PLANET, WE ARE ALL INSIGNIFICANT COMPARED TO THE VASTNESS OF THE UNIVERSE. WE ARE ALL ESSENTIALLY EQUAL. WE ARE NOT ALONE AND ISOLATED: WHEN YOU HURT SOMEONE, YOU HURT YOURSELF; WHEN YOU HELP SOMEONE, YOU HELP YOURSELF."

When he was up in space, looking down at the planet we call home, Marco realized how much we need each other. No matter what arguments or fights we may have, we are all still stuck together on one rock, floating out in endless space.

DAWN PRINCE-HUGHES

(BORN 1964)

At school, Dawn realized that she thought differently than everyone else. The other kids called her weird and she struggled to make friends. One day, she pretended to be a dog, because she thought that it would make everyone like her. Instead, everyone laughed and the teacher threw her out of the classroom.

Dawn ran away from home at the age of fifteen. For some time, she was homeless. Then she started going to Seattle's Woodland Park Zoo, spending hours watching the silverback gorillas. She was amazed by how they argued and made up, built nests, and stuck together as a group. Their directness reminded Dawn of how she saw the world.

Wanting to spend more time with the gorillas, Dawn applied to college to take a course in zoology. She completed her work while helping out at the zoo. After getting her first degree, Dawn traveled to Switzerland to do even more research.

She returned to America, wrote numerous books, met her wife, and had a son. At the age of thirty-eight, Dawn was diagnosed with autism. She came to understand that it was the reason behind why she'd seemed to think so differently to everyone at school. But Dawn doesn't think she's the only one. She's said:

"WE ARE ALL STRANGE AND BROKEN AND BEAUTIFUL IN OUR OWN WAYS. WE ARE EACH SO AFRAID OF DISCONNECTION AND YET IT CAN'T BE EASILY ESCAPED; SOME SAY IT IS AN INEVITABLE STATE OF BEING AND, PERHAPS, THE PRICE OF CONSCIOUSNESS. THAT FACT MAKES OUR CONNECTIONS TO OTHER LIVING THINGS ALL THE MORE IMPORTANT TO CULTIVATE. THERE IS BEAUTY IN OUR DIFFERENCE AND ALSO BEAUTY IN OUR SAMENESS: SAMENESS WITH OTHER ANIMALS, SAMENESS WITH ONE ANOTHER."

When Dawn ran away from home, it was because other kids had bullied her for being different. She came to realize that her differences were exactly what made her such a remarkable person. By observing the gorillas, she also learned that as different as we may be, we still all belong to one big family.

MARCUS RASHFORD
(BORN 1997)

Marcus's mom did everything she could to bring up her five children alone. Even though she worked more than one job, there wasn't always enough money to feed everyone.

The older Marcus got, the more it became clear that he had an incredible talent for soccer. He'd loved kicking a ball around ever since he was two. By the age of seven, he was playing for the Manchester United Academy, but it was difficult for him to get to practices because his mom had to work so much.

When Marcus was eleven, he became the youngest person ever to be offered a place on the Manchester United School-boy Scholars scheme. His mom was happy about him going because it meant he could stay near the ground and would be fed well by the soccer club.

From there, Marcus would go on to become one of the best-known soccer players in Britain. He has scored count-less goals for Manchester United, helped win the FA Cup, and played for England during the 2018 World Cup. But Marcus isn't only impressive on the pitch.

During the coronavirus pandemic, when schools across the UK closed, millions of children living in poverty were faced with not being able to have the free school meals they usually received. The govern-ment said they weren't going to keep providing food for those children while they were at home.

There was no way Marcus was going to let that happen. He knew exactly how it felt to go to bed hungry and he wasn't about to let so many kids feel that way too, especially during a global crisis. Marcus started working with an organization to provide food for kids who needed it, raising over twenty million pounds to do so. Eventually, because of Marcus's work, the government changed their position and agreed to keep providing free school meals for families living in poverty. Marcus wants all kids to know that:

"YOUR VOICE, YOUR STANCE, YOUR FAMILY, YOUR COMMUNITY, AND FRIENDS, ALL MATTER . . . PLEASE, NEVER GO TO BED FEELING LIKE YOU DON'T HAVE A ROLE TO PLAY IN THIS LIFE BECAUSE, BELIEVE ME WHEN I TELL YOU, THE POSSIBILITIES ARE ENDLESS."

RAINER MARIA RILKE

(1875–1926)

Rainer hated school. He'd been sent to a military academy by his father and there was nowhere in the world that would have made him less happy. Rainer was ill a lot and he missed his mother. The teachers saw his sensitivity as a weakness. He didn't fit in with the other boys; they called him names, laughed at him, and physically attacked him. Through all the pain, the dream of becoming a poet started to grow inside Rainer.

Once he was old enough to escape school, Rainer blossomed. He traveled the world, encountering magnificent artworks in the galleries in France, wild landscapes in the hinterlands of Russia, and enthralling people in the bars and universities of Europe. Inspired by everything he'd seen, Rainer wrote many poems that are still treasured by people today.

In 1902, Rainer received a letter from a nineteen-year-old student who was also studying at a military school while dreaming of becoming a poet. He wanted advice on life, love, and writing. Of course, Rainer recognized himself in the young man and gladly wrote back to him.

Over the following years, Rainer found the time to write to that student often, reading his poems and offering him all the advice he could. In one letter, Rainer gave the young poet some guidance about how we might think of those things and people that scare us most, whether they're school bullies or mythical creatures:

"HOW CAN WE FORGET THOSE ANCIENT MYTHS FOUND AT THE BEGINNINGS OF ALL PEOPLES? THE MYTHS ABOUT THE DRAGONS WHO AT THE LAST MOMENT TURN INTO PRINCESSES? PERHAPS ALL THE DRAGONS OF OUR LIVES ARE PRINCESSES, ONLY WAITING FOR THE DAY WHEN THEY WILL SEE US HANDSOME AND BRAVE? PERHAPS EVERYTHING TERRIFYING IS DEEP DOWN A HELPLESS THING THAT NEEDS OUR HELP."

ADI ROCHE

(BORN 1955)

On April 26, 1986, there was an explosion at a nuclear plant in Chernobyl, Russia. Dangerous nuclear radiation spread through the air and rain. While people couldn't feel it, smell it, or get rid of it, the radiation could cause illnesses like cancer and would stay in their bodies for life. The neighboring communities were quickly evacuated from the towns and villages around the power plant. It was too late: the radiation had spread.

Adi was living over 1,800 miles away in Ireland when the Chernobyl disaster took place. She was heartbroken by the reports she heard. To try and help, Adi created a foundation called Chernobyl Children International, which wanted to provide aid to the children who had been affected by the disaster. Adi believes that:

"WE ULTIMATELY FIND WHO WE ARE AS HUMAN BEINGS THROUGH WHAT WE CAN DO WITH AND FOR OTHERS."

Since 1991, CCI has helped over 25,000 children come from Russia and Belarus to Ireland for medical help. It has raised over 100 million dollars, built houses for families, and helped find loving homes for children living in orphanages.

Even decades after the disaster took place, its effects are still being felt. Some people who came into contact with the radiation gave birth to children who have disabilities and illnesses. Adi has not forgotten them. She continues to reach out and do everything she can for the children who are still suffering because of what happened that day.

In 2016, her campaigning meant that April 26 is now known around the world as International Chernobyl Disaster Remembrance Day. Adi discovered who she is as a person long before that; she is someone who has dedicated her life to helping the children of Chernobyl.

RUMI

(1207–1273)

Despite living over 700 years ago, there is a poet who still has fans all over the world. Rumi's poems top bestseller lists, have been performed by Hollywood's biggest stars, and are written on everything from posters to pencil cases. People turn to them for advice, for inspiration, and for a way of understanding the world around us.

Rumi was born in 1207, in a place that is now part of Afghanistan. When Genghis Khan and his Mongols invaded Central Asia, Rumi's family fled west. They passed through Baghdad, Persia, and Mecca, before finally settling in Konya, a city in the country we now call Turkey.

It was clear Rumi was clever and he became well known as a scholar and a teacher of Islam. His life took a dramatic turn, however, when Rumi met a man called Shams Tabrizi. Shams had chosen to live a simple, poor life, so that he could be closer to God. Rumi found him hugely inspiring. In fact, he found his new friend so entrancing that his students became jealous and killed Shams.

Rumi's sadness over the death of his friend didn't lead to him seeking revenge. Instead, it inspired him to write poetry. He would pen over 40,000 verses in memory of his friend and these verses are now recognized as one of the greatest works of Persian literature

ever produced. Rumi once wrote that you should:

"RAISE YOUR WORDS, NOT VOICE. IT IS RAIN THAT GROWS FLOWERS, NOT THUNDER."

In his poems, Rumi spoke about accepting all religions, accepting all people, and marveled at how strange and full of wonder life is. He wanted to spread joy and hope. The beauty of his words meant that people from many different religions came to be followers and admirers of Rumi. When he died, there were not just Muslims, but Jews, Greeks, Christians, and Persians at his funeral. They all wanted to pay their respects to the man who had used his words to grow so many beautiful flowers.

You are not a drop
in the ocean.
You are the entire
ocean in a drop.

RYOKAN

(1758–1831)

There is a story that Ryokan once found three shoots of bamboo pressing up from underneath the wooden floorboards of the simple hut he called home. Ryokan didn't like to hurt any living thing, not even plants. He decided to cut three little holes in the wood so the bamboo could grow up through his house.

"Don't worry," he told the shoots. "If you grow any more, I'll cut three holes in the roof too!"

Ryokan was a Zen Buddhist monk, who lived in a shack on the snowy slopes of Mount Kagumi in Japan. He named his house "Gogō-an," which means half a scoop of rice—or half of what one man would need to eat for one day. Ryokan spent his days meditating, practicing calligraphy, and writing haiku. He sometimes wandered into nearby villages to play with the children, dance at festivals, or chat with his friends. If Ryokan ever had more than he needed, he gave it away. Once he even gave a thief his clothes, because he felt bad that the man had traveled so far to rob him and found only an empty hut.

It was a long way from the kind of life Ryokan had once seemed destined for. His father had been a wealthy merchant and the head of their village. He had expected Ryokan, his eldest son, to follow in his footsteps. But Ryokan didn't like having to constantly deal with the con-flicts of others, and instead he entered a monastery and became a monk. He then traveled all across Japan for years, studying Zen Buddhism.

When he finally settled down in Gogō-an, one of the poems Ryokan wrote said:

$$\sim\!\sim\!\sim\!\sim\!\sim\!\sim\!\sim\!\sim\!\sim\!\sim\!\sim$$

"I HAVE NOTHING TO REPORT, MY FRIENDS. IF YOU WANT TO FIND THE MEANING, STOP CHASING AFTER SO MANY THINGS."

$$\sim\!\sim\!\sim\!\sim\!\sim\!\sim\!\sim\!\sim\!\sim\!\sim\!\sim$$

Everyone who knew Ryokan said that he was always joyful and radiant. He put others before himself, never let himself grow spiteful or cruel, and didn't take life too seriously. Ryokan had come to understand that the real meaning in life didn't come from chasing after things, but from enjoying those things that are already around you.

JONAS SALK

(1914–1995)

In the 1950s, polio was one of the most feared diseases in America. It could strike anyone, anywhere, at any time. Before he became president of the United States, Franklin D. Roosevelt caught the disease and it left him paralyzed from the waist down. Margarete Steiff, the German inventor of the teddy bear, had polio as a child and spent her life in a wheelchair because of it.

Jonas Salk was one of many scientists racing to find a polio vaccine. He was the first person in his family to go to college. When he was small, he'd been terrible at sports but loved to learn, and his mother had encouraged him to believe he could one day make a difference in the world.

Jonas went about his research by isolating the polio virus in a lab, destroying it, and injecting the dead virus into his test subjects. When he realized he'd found something that might work, the biggest medical trial in history began. Jonas and his family took the vaccine, along with almost 1.8 million American children. It was a success. Jonas had discovered a vaccine for polio.

In 1952, there were over 57,000 cases of polio in the United States. Ten years later, the number was down to just a thousand.

Jonas's passion wasn't just science, but people in general. He believed that only by coming together as humans could we achieve truly great things. He once wrote:

"WHAT IS ... IMPORTANT IS THAT WE— NUMBER ONE: LEARN TO LIVE WITH EACH OTHER. NUMBER TWO: TRY TO BRING OUT THE BEST IN EACH OTHER ... THE OBJECT IS NOT TO PUT DOWN THE OTHER, BUT TO RAISE UP THE OTHER."

Jonas chose not to make any profit from the polio vaccine, even though it could have made him a very rich man. Instead, he watched as it was rolled out in countries across the globe, saving countless lives. Jonas created the Salk Institute for Biological Studies in La Jolla, California. He invited scientists of all nationalities to come and conduct research alongside him. Jonas knew that by learning to work together, they'd achieve much more than they would alone. He dedicated the rest of his life to raising others up.

SAMPA THE GREAT

(BORN 1993)

Sampa was born in Zambia, a country in the south of Africa. The women in her community chanted spiritual songs during celebrations and funerals. Sampa realized the power music had to bring people together.

One day, Sampa wandered into her cousin's room and heard a song that blew her away. It was by an American rapper named Tupac. Sampa realized that she wanted to rap too.

At the age of eighteen, Sampa decided she wanted to see the world outside of Africa. She moved to America to study and was shocked to find how racist many Americans were towards her. When she got back to Botswana, Sampa told her sister that she never wanted to leave home again. Her sister told her that if she truly wanted to be free, she had to feel able to move around the world.

So Sampa left for Australia, a country where she'd never been and didn't know anyone. She studied music engineering at university and hung out at hip-hop freestyle sessions, where she met other musicians who listened to jazz, R & B, and hip-hop. Sampa started writing and recording her own songs. Her thrilling performances, vibrant beats, and master-ful lyrics soon meant she made a name for herself in the mostly white Australian hip-hop scene.

In an interview, Sampa explained that the best advice she'd ever been given came from her dad. It was that:

"YOU BEING YOU—YOUR UNIQUENESS— IS THE MOST IMPORTANT THING, BECAUSE IT'S SUPER REFRESHING TO NOT SOUND LIKE EVERYBODY ELSE."

Sampa refused to let go of her past, her home, or her culture to blend in with the kind of music everyone else in Australia was making. She doesn't dress, sound, or rap like anyone else. She sounds like herself and people love her for it. Sampa has won countless awards, performed with the most famous hip-hop artists alive, and become an inspiration for thousands of young people. She's shown it's possible to move oceans away from the place you were born and still shine so brightly that everyone takes notice.

ROBERT SCHUMANN

(1810–1856)

As a boy, Robert saw a performance by the pianist Ignaz Moscheles, and decided that he wanted to devote his life to playing the piano too. His father supported his dream but his mother thought that he should do something more serious. When his father tragically passed away, Robert decided he would follow his mother's wishes. He moved to a German city called Heidelberg to study law.

Then, one day, a famed Italian violinist named Niccolò Paganini came to play in Germany. Robert was in the audience. That performance reminded him of how deeply he loved music. He left his law studies behind and returned to his seat in front of the piano.

But Robert injured one of his hands and it soon became clear that he would never become a virtuoso pianist like Ignaz Moscheles. He didn't let that deter him from music. Instead, Robert began to compose pieces of music for others to play. He wrote tunes inspired by scenes from his favorite stories, his personal life, and the people and places that had shaped him. Often his music would wander off into unexpected places, returning with great, bright sweeps of joy, or moments of delicate sadness.

In 1850, Robert wrote a book called *Advice to Young Musicians*, in which he said:

> "LOVE YOUR PECULIAR INSTRUMENT, BUT BE NOT VAIN ENOUGH TO CONSIDER IT THE GREATEST AND ONLY ONE. REMEMBER THAT THERE ARE OTHERS AS FINE AS YOURS."

Robert understood that each instrument, like each person, had its own voice. By learning to weave together these different sounds, he could create music that captured and provoked some of our deepest human emotions.

At the age of forty-four, Robert was suffering from difficult mental health problems. He heard angelic music that wasn't there and his moods could leap from painfully low to a manic energy. For his own safety, Robert asked to be sent to a hospital for people suffering from mental illness.

Although Robert is gone, his music is still played today in concert halls, cathedrals, and homes around the world.

IGNAZ SEMMELWEIS

(1818–1865)

With three words, Ignaz managed to save millions of lives. They were three words that other doctors laughed at him for and they were three words that you may hear a lot. Those three words were:

~~~~~~~~~~~~~~~~~~~~~~~~~~~~

"WASH YOUR HANDS."

~~~~~~~~~~~~~~~~~~~~~~~~~~~~

Ignaz passed his medical exam in 1844 and was later sent to work at Vienna General Hospital in Austria. There, he was put in the maternity ward, looking after newborn babies and the women who had just given birth to them.

But Ignaz quickly realized something was wrong. Many of the women who'd given birth were dying and there seemed to be a pattern. The women who were looked after by midwives were a lot more likely to survive than the women who were looked after by doctors and medical students. Ignaz wondered if this could be because the students and doctors were touching dead bodies as part of their studies, while the midwives only touched their patients. He decided that the doctors might be getting invisible disease particles on their hands and spreading them to the mothers, causing them to get ill and die.

It's something we now all know, but at the time it was not believed that illness could be passed around by tiny germs on our hands. In fact, the staff at the hospital were so annoyed by Ignaz's idea that they refused to extend his contract. He returned to his home city of Budapest, in Hungary, and took a job at St. Rochus Hospital. There, he made sure all of the doctors washed their hands, and soon enough, the number of deaths began to drop.

Unfortunately, Ignaz would pass away before the world realized how important his discovery was. Now all of us, not just doctors, wash our hands many times a day. Ignaz is proof that the heroes of the future are often laughed at in their own lifetimes. He showed that even when the whole world seems against you, it might be the world that's wrong, not you.

SENECA

(4 BC–65 AD)

Lucius Annaeus Seneca lived over 2,000 years ago. Although he wrote a lot about what it means to be a good person, he would end up tutoring one of the most vicious and bloodthirsty rulers who ever existed.

Many of Seneca's thoughts were part of an ancient tradition called Stoicism. The aim of Stoicism was to discover how to live a good life, how to keep your mind peaceful, and how to be a virtuous person. The Stoics believed that everyone on earth was part of one community and that we should strive to live in harmony with each other and with nature. Although it started thousands of years ago in the colonnades of Athens, the teachings of Stoicism are still popular today, with everyone from athletes to lawyers.

Seneca's first writing comes from a period when he was banished from Rome and sent to live on an island called Corsica. A new emperor had taken control of the Roman Empire and he was trying to weed out anyone he thought might stand against him. For eight years, Seneca would live on that small, rocky island, surrounded by crystal-clear waters. He had a lot of time to think.

Eventually, Seneca was allowed back to Rome in order to tutor the future emperor, Nero. Nero would become known for murdering anyone who stood in his way, persecuting Christians, and standing on his roof singing as Rome burned. When Seneca met him, he tried to pass on his teachings about everything from anger to earthquakes. He once said:

> "IT IS NOT BECAUSE THINGS ARE DIFFICULT THAT WE DO NOT DARE; IT IS BECAUSE WE DO NOT DARE THAT THINGS ARE DIFFICULT."

What Seneca wanted to point out is that while some things make us afraid because they seem hard, other things only seem hard because we are afraid of them. There are many times—whether it's in a math class, by a swimming pool, or on a stage—that if we can only find the courage to try something new, we may well find it far easier than we thought.

Nero eventually turned against his tutor and had him killed. Two thousand years later, the great philosopher's thoughts still guide people through difficult times.

CHEN SHU-CHU

(BORN 1951)

From the age of thirteen until the age of sixty-seven when she retired, Chen spent every day at her vegetable stand in Taitung Central Market, on the southeast coast of Taiwan. She would arrive early and set out taro, pumpkin, chilies, and pak choi for her customers to browse. Chen would work for up to eighteen hours a day, six days a week.

When she was still in elementary school, Chen's mother had died because the family hadn't been able to get her treatment in a hospital. Not long after that, Chen took over the vegetable stall as a way of helping her father look after Chen and her siblings.

As an adult, Chen would live off just three dollars a day and save the rest so she could donate it to those who needed her help. Her donations have helped build a school library at Jen-Ai elementary school as well as a wing of Taitung Hospital. She has also adopted three children and made many donations to charities that help the poor.

When someone asked why Chen chose to give away almost all of her money, she told them:

"LIFE IS SHORT. WE ARE BORN WITH NO MATERIAL POSSESSIONS AND SHALL DIE THE SAME WAY. MONEY IS ONLY USEFUL WHEN IT IS IN THE HANDS OF PEOPLE IN NEED."

Chen proved that you don't need to have a lot to make a big difference. In fact, as a vegetable seller in a small town in Taiwan, Chen has helped more people than many of the richest men and women on earth. She knows that money is wasted if it is only spent on fancy clothes or expensive food, and that its true value lies in the way it is able to improve the lives of the poor.

Chen's generosity didn't go unnoticed. She was named as one of *TIME*'s 100 most influential people in 2010, for which she was invited to a banquet in New York City. In 2012, Chen was given the Ramon Magsaysay Award, which came with a $50,000 prize. She immediately donated all of the money to a hospital in Taiwan.

CARL THEODOR SØRENSEN
(1893–1979)

Carl believed that kids should be able to build their own playgrounds. He thought it was boring to have play areas filled with swings and merry-go-rounds, where all kids could do was repeat the same movement, over and over again. He wanted to give young people a place where their imaginations could run wild. He wanted to create a kind of playground where kids could have real adventures.

In Carl's first playground, built in the district of Emdrup in Denmark, there was junk everywhere, and kids were free to do whatever they wanted with it. They could nail together planks of wood, pile up bricks, and dig into the dirt. They could create towers and castles. They could hide out in dens, climb trees, and chase each other through cities they'd built themselves. Carl believed his playgrounds gave children a chance to:

"DREAM AND IMAGINE AND MAKE DREAMS AND IMAGINATION REALITY."

Some people were horrified by Carl's idea and thought it was far too dangerous to let children do whatever they wanted with scrap materials. But the playground turned out to be surprisingly safe. More importantly, it gave children a place to express their creativity.

Soon people around the world were trying out the idea too. In Britain, after buildings were bombed during the Second World War, Lady Allen of Hurtwood turned some of the bomb sites into playgrounds where children could do as they pleased.

Unfortunately, worries about safety mean there aren't many junk playgrounds left. But Carl's ideas live on in the parents, teachers, and caregivers who know that if children are going to change the world, they must first be encouraged to imagine the kind of world in which they'd like to live.

FREYA STARK

(1893–1993)

On her ninth birthday, Freya was given a copy of *One Thousand and One Nights*, the famous collection of folk tales from the Middle East. It includes stories like "Aladdin," "Sinbad the Sailor," and "Ali Baba and the Forty Thieves." Freya was entranced. She swore that one day she would visit the distant countries from the stories in her book.

After serving as a nurse in Italy during the First World War, Freya traveled to London and studied Arabic at university. Once she got a grip on the language, she headed to Lebanon on her first adventure. Freya rode alone on a donkey through Syria, sleeping in the houses of friendly villagers on the way. Some people thought it was reckless and irresponsible, while others thought she was incredibly brave. It would be the first of many incredible journeys Freya would make.

Unlike most of the other visitors who came to the Middle East from the West, Freya didn't travel with servants or insist on riding by horse. Instead, she got to know the locals, learned their languages, and traveled alongside them. Freya knew that the way to truly understand a culture was to form real relationships with the people who belonged to it.

Freya wrote many books about her travels. At a time when few women had the freedom to set off on their own adventures, Freya proved it was possible. In one book, *The Lycian Shore*, she wrote:

"THERE CAN BE NO HAPPINESS IF THE THINGS WE BELIEVE IN ARE DIFFERENT FROM THE THINGS WE DO."

Through all her escapades, she had come to realize that we have to be true to ourselves if we're ever going to be content. If you believe in kindness, you must practice kindness. If you believe in riding out into the desert on a donkey, then you must ride out into the desert on a donkey. When we behave in ways that don't match our beliefs, we get lost. If we want to be happy, then we must try to act in ways that make ourselves proud.

JUNKO TABEI

(1939–2016)

When Junko was ten, a schoolteacher took her class for a hike up Mount Nasu, a group of volcanoes in Japan's Nikko National Park. It was a tough climb, up steep slopes of sand and rock, past a burbling stream of hot water, to the cool, quiet summit. Even though many adults thought of her as a weak child, Junko fell in love with climbing that day.

Growing up, Junko planned to become a teacher but climbing was never far from her mind. At the time, the only climbing clubs that existed in Japan were for men. Junko joined one anyway, ignoring the moans and grumbles of the male climbers. She eventually founded the Joshi-Tohan Club, a mountaineering club for women. She climbed every large mountain in Japan and paid for her adventures by working as an editor for a science magazine, giving piano lessons, and teaching English.

As much as she learned about climbing, Junko knew that knowledge alone wasn't enough to get you anywhere. She once said:

"TECHNIQUE AND ABILITY ALONE DO NOT GET YOU TO THE TOP;

IT IS THE WILLPOWER THAT IS MOST IMPORTANT."

This proved especially true when Junko embarked on her expedition to climb Everest, the earth's highest mountain. She was only the thirty-eighth person ever to manage the climb, and the first woman to complete it. It wasn't easy. Of the eight climbers who set out on the journey, only Junko made it to the top. She continued even after an avalanche buried her tent and she had to be dug out by the native Sherpa guides.

In 2019, a mountain range on Pluto was named after Junko. It is a testament to the woman who kept going no matter what. She knew that sheer determination is the only way to reach such dizzying heights.

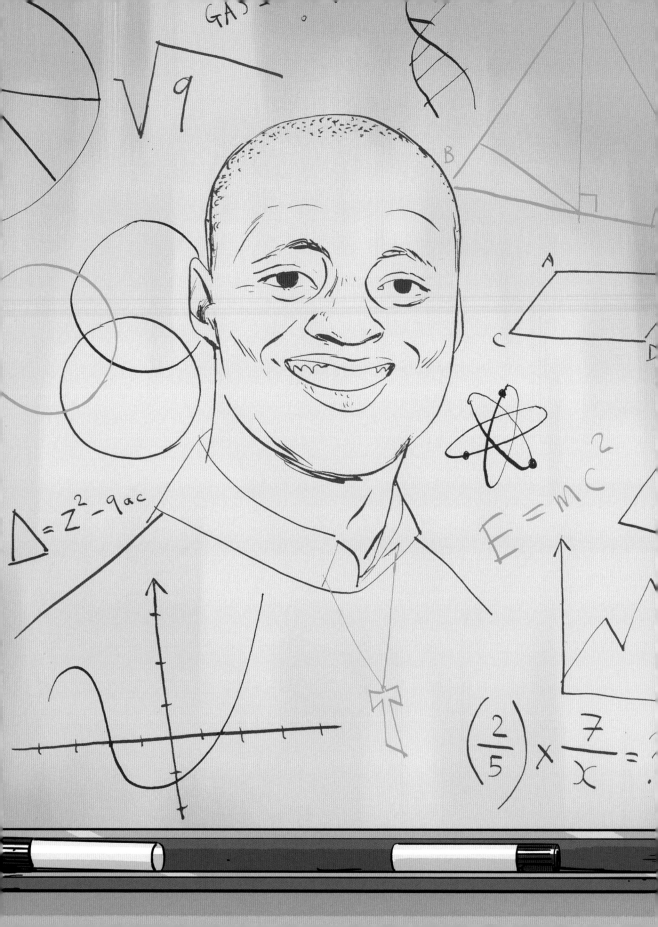

BROTHER PETER TABICHI
(BORN 1982)

Peter is a science teacher at Keriko Mixed Day Secondary School in Pwani, Kenya. The school has one desktop computer, very few textbooks, and fifty-eight students to every teacher. Most of the pupils are very poor, many are orphans, and a lot of them have to walk four miles on rough roads just to get to school.

Despite these difficulties, Peter does everything he can to ensure his students receive a decent education. He uses 80 percent of his small salary to buy uniforms, supplies, and food for the poorest children. He downloads information in internet cafés, takes photos on his phone, and searches for materials and objects that he can use to improve his lessons. He also started a peace club at the school to try and bring together children from different tribes, genders, and villages. Members of the peace club work together to plant trees, debate, and play sports—activities that unite them.

Peter's efforts are working. The number of students at Keriko Secondary School has doubled since Peter joined and the number of kids who go on to study at college and university has gone up dramatically. Science projects put together by Peter's students, like one where electricity was produced by plants, have seen them give presentations in America and receive scholarships that enable them to go to college. Peter believes that:

〰〰〰〰〰〰〰〰〰〰〰〰

"EVERYONE HAS THEIR POTENTIAL TO CHANGE THE WORLD. WE WERE CREATED FOR A REASON AND TO BE HAPPY. WE CAN WORK TOWARDS HAPPINESS, BUT ALL OF US NEED TO DO OUR PART SO THAT THE WORLD BECOMES A BETTER PLACE."

〰〰〰〰〰〰〰〰〰〰〰〰

In 2019, Peter won the Global Teacher Prize, given by the Varkey Foundation. The prize awarded him one million dollars, which he'll use to continue improving the lives of his students, his community, and all of the communities around them. He wants to find a way of using the money to help as many people as possible. He's going to use it to change the world.

GRETA THUNBERG

(BORN 2003)

In 2018, Sweden experienced its hottest summer
for over 250 years. Wildfires were consuming forests and
whole villages had to be evacuated. Greta turned fifteen
that year but she had been learning about climate change
since she was eight. She had come to understand that
the actions of people out to make money were heating
up the planet and destroying the environment.

Greta had been diagnosed with Asperger's syndrome and selective mutism, which means she sometimes finds social communication difficult and only speaks when she thinks it's really necessary. Seeing what was happening to her country, Greta knew it was time to raise her voice. For almost three weeks, she didn't go to school. Instead she sat outside the Swedish government building with a sign that read "School Strike for Climate."

Soon, word of Greta's protest began to spread. TV channels, blogs, and social media accounts reposted her message. Greta gave public speeches about how sad and angry she was that the people in charge of the world had failed to protect it. She inspired thousands of other students from across the world to strike from school and demanded that the adults with power start to take responsibility for the environment.

Greta's message for other young people is that:

> "YOU MUST UNITE BEHIND THE SCIENCE. YOU MUST TAKE ACTION. YOU MUST DO THE IMPOSSIBLE. BECAUSE GIVING UP CAN NEVER EVER BE AN OPTION."

What began as one girl, in one country, holding one sign, became a movement that spread across the globe. Politicians have made promises, students have gone on strike, and millions of people have made pledges to stop flying on airplanes. Greta is proof that one person taking action can lead to a whole planet waking up to the crisis that is threatening their world.

DESMOND TUTU

(BORN 1931)

When Desmond was young, he contracted polio.
Although he was lucky enough to recover, Desmond's
right hand would remain withered and weak.

Conditions in his neighborhood in the North West Province of South Africa were dirty and difficult. There were open sewers and almost none of the makeshift houses had running water. Desmond and his friends made toys for themselves out of old wires.

When Desmond was seventeen, the racist political group, the National Party, gained power of South Africa. Despite only making up 20 percent of the population, the white rulers took almost 90 percent of the land for themselves. They also created laws that forbade black people from mixing with white people and denied them many basic rights, like being able to get a good education, marry who they wanted, vote, or own land. This kind of racist separation was called apartheid.

At Desmond's college, apartheid was in full force. He and other black students were subjected to abuse from white students and made to sleep in grass huts, while the white students lived in brick buildings.

After completing his studies, Desmond became a teacher but quit to protest the way black students were treated. He joined the church instead, eventually becoming the Archbishop of Cape Town.

Desmond gave rousing speeches, led marches, and pleaded for peace. Despite the horror that Desmond and other black South Africans experienced at the hands of the white government, he refused to let hate into his heart. He knew that fury would only lead to more violence. What Desmond wanted to do was remind all of his countrymen that we are all one people.

In the introduction to a book on forgiveness, Desmond explained his view by saying:

"WE ARE MADE FOR GOODNESS. WE ARE MADE FOR LOVE. WE ARE MADE FOR FRIENDLINESS. WE ARE MADE FOR TOGETHERNESS. ... WE ARE MADE TO TELL THE WORLD THAT THERE ARE NO OUTSIDERS. ALL ARE WELCOME: BLACK, WHITE, RED, YELLOW, RICH, POOR, EDUCATED, NOT EDUCATED, MALE, FEMALE, GAY, STRAIGHT, ALL, ALL, ALL. WE ALL BELONG TO THIS FAMILY, THIS HUMAN FAMILY, GOD'S FAMILY."

UNITED NATIONS GENERAL ASSEMBLY

(FOUNDED 1945)

In 1945, the devastating effects of two world wars were being felt around the globe. Millions were dead, millions more were homeless, and countless towns and cities had been destroyed. An organization was founded that would aim to keep peace between the countries of the world and try to prevent any such horrors from occurring again. This organization was named the United Nations.

The first meeting of the United Nations took place in London in 1946. There, representatives from fifty-one different countries came together to discuss and debate how to deal with all the issues that came up between them.

In 1948, it was decided that the United Nations ought to set out in words the rights that every human being was entitled to. They wanted to create a document that could be used to measure whether the behavior of a country or its leaders was right or wrong. It was called the Universal Declaration of Human Rights. Its very first article reads:

"ALL HUMAN BEINGS ARE BORN FREE AND EQUAL IN DIGNITY AND RIGHTS. THEY ARE ENDOWED WITH REASON AND CONSCIENCE AND SHOULD ACT TOWARDS ONE ANOTHER IN A SPIRIT OF BROTHERHOOD."

The document goes on to explain that everyone—no matter their age, religion, skin color, gender, sexuality, or nationality—should be entitled to freedom, housing, healthcare, and fair treatment by the law.

The United Nations was born out of a time in human history when it had become very clear what could happen when we stop acting towards each other in a spirit of brotherhood. It now has 193 members. Every year in September, the United Nations General Assembly meet in New York City to look for ways to keep peace in the world and fight for those who have had their rights taken from them.

GIANNI VERSACE

(1946–1997)

Gianni was nine years old when he made his first dress. He'd spent countless hours watching his mother sew in her workshop and had finally decided it was his turn.

After finishing school, Gianni worked with his mother for a while before moving to Milan to follow his dream of becoming a fashion designer. He formed a company with his brother and sister and got to work building the fashion empire that would make his name known around the world.

In the design of his clothes, Gianni combined the themes and symbols of the ancient cultures of Italy with bold, bright, modern styles. He created shirts, trousers, and dresses that amazed and inspired fashion-lovers everywhere. More importantly, he created clothes that people wanted to wear. Clothes that made them feel brave and strong and confident. Clothes that allowed them to express themselves.

One of Gianni's most famous dresses was held together entirely by safety pins. Many were made of a fabric called Oroton, which was a kind of glitzy, glamorous silky version of the chain mail that warriors once wore. Gianni had invented Oroton himself.

Some critics thought Gianni's clothes were too shocking. Gianni didn't care.

He knew that anyone who dares to do anything different will be faced with people who don't like what they're doing. His advice on fashion?

"DON'T BE INTO TRENDS. DON'T MAKE FASHION OWN YOU, BUT YOU DECIDE WHAT YOU ARE, WHAT YOU WANT TO EXPRESS BY THE WAY YOU DRESS AND THE WAY TO LIVE."

Tragically, Gianni was killed when he was just fifty, but his vision still lives on. Gianni proved that fashion is about more than just clothes; it's about who we are and how we want to live. Fashion shouldn't be about following trends; it should be about expressing yourself without being afraid of what others might think.

ELIZABETH WANJIRU WATHUTI

(BORN 1995)

At the age of seven, Elizabeth planted her first seed. She comes from Nyeri County, in Kenya, an area known for rolling hills covered in lush green trees. When Elizabeth learned about how many similar forests around the world were being destroyed, she became determined to do something to help. She started a club at her school for people who wanted to fight to protect the environment.

Elizabeth doesn't think you're ever too young to make a difference:

-- -- -- -- -- -- -- -- -- -- -- --

"AS YOUNG PEOPLE, WE CAN CHANGE THE FUTURE OF SOCIETY BY DEMONSTRATING COURAGEOUS BEHAVIOR ... WE ARE THE BACK-BONE OF EVERY NATION AND ARE THE FUTURE LEADERS. THIS MESSAGE IS EMPOWERING BUT BRINGS WITH IT GREAT RESPONSIBILITY. AS YOUNG LEADERS, WE SHOULD THEREFORE ALWAYS AIM TO BE ACCOUNTABLE FOR OUR ACTIONS, AND IN PARTICULAR BE AWARE THAT POOR ENVIRONMENTAL DECISIONS WILL GREATLY AFFECT FUTURE GENERATIONS ..."

-- -- -- -- -- -- -- -- -- -- -- --

Elizabeth started the Green Generation Initiative to encourage young people to fight back against the forces that are laying waste to nature. She travels around Kenya, giving school talks about climate change and planting new trees side-by-side with the students. As Elizabeth tells the children she meets, trees are one of the best defenses we have against climate change because they can absorb a lot of the carbon dioxide gas that is heating up our planet.

Elizabeth has now planted over 30,000 trees in her home country of Kenya. She's even created her own tree nursery, so that she can grow her own seedlings and not have to buy them. More than anything, Elizabeth wants people to understand just how much we rely on nature. If we keep hurting the natural world, then we'll end up hurting ourselves too.

PATRICK WEIL

(BORN 1956)

When disaster strikes a community, it is hoped that governments and charities will rush in to provide food, shelter, and clothing for the people worst affected by it. Patrick feels there is something else that is needed too:

> **"PEOPLE WHO HAVE LOST EVERYTHING NEED BOOKS, FILMS, GAMES, AND INTERNET ACCESS TO FEED THEIR MINDS, CONNECT WITH LOVED ONES, PURSUE EDUCATION, AND REBUILD THEIR LIVES."**

Patrick knows that access to stories and knowledge is vital for those suffering from tragedy to find hope. It's not enough to have food in our bellies and roofs over our heads; we need ways of learning about the world, understanding ourselves, and escaping on magical adventures. If you're stuck in a place that isn't home, afraid and unsure of what tomorrow might hold, stories can be a way for you to imagine a future.

That's why Patrick started Libraries Without Borders. The organization aims to bring books, films, games, and the internet to people around the world who find themselves living in refugee camps. At first, it was a tiny charity, run out of Patrick's house. Now, Libraries Without Borders is huge.

Every year, Libraries Without Borders sends out over 100,000 books to almost half a million readers. It supports the building of libraries and schools, arranges story times for children in camps, and helps train local people as librarians. Some of the libraries are physical, while others are digital. They have also launched bookmobiles: brightly painted trucks and buses that can bring books to children living in isolated regions.

One of their most successful projects has been the Ideas Box, which is a large, colorful crate that opens to provide everything you need to set up a library: tables, chairs, tablets, 50,000 e-books, 250 printed books, four laptops, board games, and a projector with 100 films to watch on it. The box even provides internet access and has its own source of energy.

Patrick knows that without education, children might never learn what they're capable of. He's determined to give young people books so that they feel empowered to take charge of their stories.

MELATI & ISABEL WIJSEN

(BORN 2001 & 2003)

Melati and Isabel grew up on the beautiful Indonesian island of Bali. Their home had crystal-clear waters, beaches of white sand, and lush hilltops cloaked in green forest. It also had a huge problem with plastic bags.

During a lesson at school, Isabel and Melati discovered that Bali produced enough plastic trash to fill a fourteen-story building, every single day. Most plastic bags were not recycled. Instead, they would end up as litter, washed into rivers and carried out to the ocean.

The two sisters decided that they would fight to get plastic bags banned from their island. It seemed like a daunting task, especially when the girls were just ten and twelve years old. But they believed in their own power. Isabel once said:

"TO ALL THE KIDS OF THIS BEAUTIFUL BUT CHALLENGING WORLD: GO FOR IT! MAKE THAT DIFFERENCE. WE'RE NOT TELLING YOU IT'S GOING TO BE EASY. WE'RE TELLING YOU IT'S GOING TO BE WORTH IT."

The sisters named their campaign Bye Bye Plastic Bags. Their first step was building a huge network of kids, schools, and organizations across Bali. They held festivals, organized beach cleanups, and gave out sustainable bags made of netting, paper, and canvas. It still wasn't enough to make the government listen, but the girls weren't about to give up.

They decided to collect one million signatures. This might have looked impossible, until the girls realized that sixteen million people passed through Bali airport every year. Eventually, they were able to find the manager of the airport, knock on his front door, and convince him to let them collect signatures from arriving travelers.

The girls then decided to go on a hunger strike. Although a full strike would be too dangerous, the sisters spoke to a nutritionist and came to an agreement: until the mayor of Bali agreed to speak to them, they would not eat between sunrise and sunset.

Eventually, he did, and plastic bags were banned across Bali. The two young sisters proved that they were capable of making a huge difference to the island that they call home. It hadn't been easy, but it was more than worth it. The government of Bali has now pledged to ensure that all of the plastics on the island are recyclable or reusable by 2025.

MARGUERITE YOURCENAR

(1903–1987)

In 1981, Marguerite became the first woman ever to be elected to the French Academy, an exclusive club dedicated to discussions about the French language. It has existed since 1635 and can only ever have forty members at one time. Some people say that when she joined, they changed the bathroom signs so that one read "Gentlemen" and the other read "Marguerite Yourcenar."

As a girl, Marguerite would sit for hours with her father, passing books back and forth as they read. When Marguerite started writing, they came up with her pen name together: Yourcenar is an anagram of her original surname, Crayencour. Her father sent her stories out to publishers on her behalf.

One afternoon, Marguerite was sitting outside a café in Paris with a friend, discussing the poetry of Samuel Taylor Coleridge. An American woman came over and told them that they had understood his poetry all wrong. Marguerite fell in love with that woman. Her name was Grace, and Marguerite soon found herself sailing across the Atlantic Ocean so that they could be together. The two of them bought a house on a wild, rugged island called Mount Desert Island.

From their home on the island, Marguerite wrote and wrote. In her most well-known novel, *The Memoirs of Hadrian*, she told the life story of the Roman Emperor Hadrian, who built a wall all the way across Britain, reconstructed the majestic Pantheon, and founded new cities in Egypt, Asia, and Greece. It was an unusual, ambitious book that became an immediate hit.

Marguerite once wrote:

"WE WOULD ALL BE TRANSFORMED IF WE HAD THE COURAGE TO BE WHO WE ARE."

Marguerite knew how many people spend their lives pretending to be people that they aren't. She refused to pretend. She loved who she wanted to love, wrote what she wanted to write, and said what she wanted to say. It was precisely because she had the courage to be who she was that Marguerite became such a cherished and respected writer on both sides of the Atlantic Ocean.

MALALA YOUSAFZAI

(BORN 1997)

When an extremist group called the Taliban took control of Malala's town in Pakistan, they banned music, forbade TVs, and declared that girls were no longer allowed to receive an education. Malala's father ran a school for girls. She knew how important education is in shaping the lives of young people. To fight back against the Taliban, Malala continued going to school, gave speeches, and wrote a blog for the BBC.

One day, while she was traveling home from school, a member of the Taliban climbed on to Malala's bus, armed with a gun. He asked which girl was Malala. Without thinking, her friends looked in her direction and the extremist shot Malala in the head. Miraculously, she survived. She was airlifted to a hospital in the UK for emergency surgery.

Malala would go on to call England her home. She has used it as a base while she keeps fighting for the rights of children around the globe. In 2013, Malala delivered a speech to the UN General Assembly on the rights of children, saying:

〰〰〰〰〰〰〰〰〰〰

"DEAR BROTHERS AND SISTERS, WE MUST NOT FORGET THAT MILLIONS OF PEOPLE ARE SUFFERING FROM POVERTY AND INJUSTICE AND IGNORANCE. WE MUST NOT FORGET

THAT MILLIONS OF CHILDREN ARE OUT OF THEIR SCHOOLS. WE MUST NOT FORGET THAT OUR SISTERS AND BROTHERS ARE WAITING FOR A BRIGHT, PEACEFUL FUTURE."

〰〰〰〰〰〰〰〰〰〰

Malala became a symbol of resistance and hope for people everywhere. She has also refused to let the world forget just how many children are suffering. Though many of us live in countries where life is not so dangerous and education is taken for granted, we have to remember that not everyone is so lucky. As Malala has said, we have to help our brothers and sisters who don't have access to the same rights and freedoms as we do.

At seventeen years old, Malala became the youngest person to be awarded the Nobel Peace Prize. Her birthday, July 12, was declared Malala Day.

LIN YUTANG

(1895–1976)

There are over 50,000 different characters in the Chinese language (although you would only need to know about 2,500 to read a newspaper). This meant that creating a Chinese typewriter was an incredibly difficult task. The English typewriter was invented in 1874, but by the 1940s, there was still no Chinese equivalent.

Lin set out to change that. He'd always been fascinated by language, from his school years spent among the green mountains of Banzai, China, to his time wandering the endless libraries of Harvard in the US. Lin was in awe of the power words had to influence people and he wanted to come up with a machine capable of harnessing that power.

By devising a set of seventy-two special keys, Lin managed to create the very first Chinese typewriter, capable of producing up to 7,000 different characters. Lin also translated numerous Chinese books into English and put together a Chinese-English dictionary, opening a channel of communication between two cultures. Lin wrote his own books too, many of which included his thoughts and wisdom, such as:

"THE SECRET OF CONTENTMENT IS KNOWING HOW TO ENJOY WHAT YOU HAVE, AND TO BE ABLE TO LOSE ALL DESIRE FOR THINGS BEYOND YOUR REACH."

Lin brought stories of the real China to people living in the West, at a time when few people knew very much about this distant country. He formed a bridge between the two cultures. Even when the government of China became angry at him for believing that literature was a way of expressing yourself, rather than of glorifying your country, Lin refused to bow to the pressure.

As a result, Lin spent most of his later life living abroad, in America and Germany. Everywhere he went, Lin couldn't understand why so many people seemed to devote themselves almost entirely to work they didn't enjoy. To him, the ideal society would be one in which people had the time and freedom to appreciate the world around them. He knew that the key to happiness didn't lie in getting more, but in getting better at appreciating what you already have.

Ben Brooks was born in 1992 and lives in Berlin. He is the author of several books, including *Grow Up* and *Lolito*, which won the Somerset Maugham Award in 2015. He is the author of the international bestsellers *Stories for Boys Who Dare To Be Different* and *Stories for Kids Who Dare To Be Different* as well as the parenting guide *Things They Don't Want You to Know*.

Quinton Winter is the illustrator of the award-winning international bestsellers *Stories for Boys Who Dare to be Different* and *Stories for Kids Who Dare to be Different*. His drawings have featured in newspapers, magazines, and children's books. He is also the illustrator of *Monsters – 100 Weird Creatures from Around the World* by Sarah Banville.